OPPOSING VIEWPOINTS® SERIES

Poverty, Prosperity, and the Minimum Wage

Other Books of Related Interest

Opposing Viewpoints Series

Automation of Labor
Gentrification and the Housing Crisis
Labor Unions and Workers' Rights
Uber, Lyft, Airbnb, and the Sharing Economy
The Wealth Gap

At Issue Series

Environmental Racism and Classism
The Federal Budget and Government Spending
Food Security
The Right to a Living Wage
Student Debt

Current Controversies Series

Are There Two Americas?
Domestic vs. Offshore Manufacturing
Fair Trade
The Gig Economy
Learned Helplessness, Welfare, and the Poverty Cycle

Poverty, Prosperity, and the Minimum Wage

Avery Elizabeth Hurt, Book Editor

GREENHAVEN
PUBLISHING

Published in 2022 by Greenhaven Publishing, LLC
353 3rd Avenue, Suite 255, New York, NY 10010

Articles in Greenhaven Publishing anthologies are often edited for length to meet page
requirements. In addition, original titles of these works are changed to clearly present
the main thesis and to explicitly indicate the author's opinion. Every effort is made to
ensure that Greenhaven Publishing accurately reflects the original intent of the authors.
Every effort has been made to trace the owners of the copyrighted material.

Cover image: J. J. Gouin/Shutterstock.com

Library of Congress Cataloging-in-Publication Data

Names: Hurt, Avery Elizabeth, editor.
Title: Poverty, prosperity, and the minimum wage / Avery Elizabeth Hurt,
    book editor.
Description: First edition. | New York : Greenhaven Publishing, 2022. |
    Series: Opposing viewpoints | Includes bibliographical references and
    index. | Contents: Poverty, prosperity, and the minimum wage | Audience:
    Ages 15+ | Audience: Grades 10–12 | Summary: "Anthology of diverse
    viewpoints exploring stagnating wages in the United States and how an
    increase to the federal minimum wage would affect workers and the
    economy"— Provided by publisher.
Identifiers: LCCN 2021042086 | ISBN 9781534508477 (library binding) | ISBN
    9781534508460 (paperback)
Subjects: LCSH: Minimum wage—United States—Juvenile literature. |
    Poverty—United States—Juvenile literature. | United States—Economic
    conditions—Juvenile literature.
Classification: LCC HD4918 .P68 2022 | DDC 331.2/3—dc23
LC record available at https://lccn.loc.gov/2021042086

Manufactured in the United States of America

Website: http://greenhavenpublishing.com

Contents

Chapter 3: Would Raising the Minimum Wage Harm Businesses?

Chapter 4: Is Raising the Minimum Wage a Moral Imperative?

The Importance of Opposing Viewpoints

P erhaps every generation experiences a period in time in which the populace seems especially polarized, starkly divided on the important issues of the day and gravitating toward the far ends of the political spectrum and away from a consensus-facilitating middle ground. The world that today's students are growing up in and that they will soon enter into as active and engaged citizens is deeply fragmented in just this way. Issues relating to terrorism, immigration, women's rights, minority rights, race relations, health care, taxation, wealth and poverty, the environment, policing, military intervention, the proper role of government—in some ways, perennial issues that are freshly and uniquely urgent and vital with each new generation—are currently roiling the world.

If we are to foster a knowledgeable, responsible, active, and engaged citizenry among today's youth, we must provide them with the intellectual, interpretive, and critical-thinking tools and experience necessary to make sense of the world around them and of the all-important debates and arguments that inform it. After all, the outcome of these debates will in large measure determine the future course, prospects, and outcomes of the world and its peoples, particularly its youth. If they are to become successful members of society and productive and informed citizens, students need to learn how to evaluate the strengths and weaknesses of someone else's arguments, how to sift fact from opinion and fallacy, and how to test the relative merits and validity of their own opinions against the known facts and the best possible available information. The landmark series Opposing Viewpoints has been providing students with just such critical-thinking skills and exposure to the debates surrounding society's most urgent contemporary issues for many years, and it continues to serve this essential role with undiminished commitment, care, and rigor.

The key to the series's success in achieving its goal of sharpening students' critical-thinking and analytic skills resides in its title—

Opposing Viewpoints. In every intriguing, compelling, and engaging volume of this series, readers are presented with the widest possible spectrum of distinct viewpoints, expert opinions, and informed argumentation and commentary, supplied by some of today's leading academics, thinkers, analysts, politicians, policy makers, economists, activists, change agents, and advocates. Every opinion and argument anthologized here is presented objectively and accorded respect. There is no editorializing in any introductory text or in the arrangement and order of the pieces. No piece is included as a "straw man," an easy ideological target for cheap point-scoring. As wide and inclusive a range of viewpoints as possible is offered, with no privileging of one particular political ideology or cultural perspective over another. It is left to each individual reader to evaluate the relative merits of each argument— as he or she sees it, and with the use of ever-growing critical-thinking skills—and grapple with his or her own assumptions, beliefs, and perspectives to determine how convincing or successful any given argument is and how the reader's own stance on the issue may be modified or altered in response to it.

This process is facilitated and supported by volume, chapter, and selection introductions that provide readers with the essential context they need to begin engaging with the spotlighted issues, with the debates surrounding them, and with their own perhaps shifting or nascent opinions on them. In addition, guided reading and discussion questions encourage readers to determine the authors' point of view and purpose, interrogate and analyze the various arguments and their rhetoric and structure, evaluate the arguments' strengths and weaknesses, test their claims against available facts and evidence, judge the validity of the reasoning, and bring into clearer, sharper focus the reader's own beliefs and conclusions and how they may differ from or align with those in the collection or those of their classmates.

Research has shown that reading comprehension skills improve dramatically when students are provided with compelling, intriguing, and relevant "discussable" texts. The subject matter of these collections could not be more compelling, intriguing, or urgently relevant to today's students and the world they are poised to inherit. The anthologized articles and the reading and discussion questions that are included with them also provide the basis for stimulating, lively, and passionate classroom debates. Students who are compelled to anticipate objections to their own argument and identify the flaws in those of an opponent read more carefully, think more critically, and steep themselves in relevant context, facts, and information more thoroughly. In short, using discussable text of the kind provided by every single volume in the Opposing Viewpoints series encourages close reading, facilitates reading comprehension, fosters research, strengthens critical thinking, and greatly enlivens and energizes classroom discussion and participation. The entire learning process is deepened, extended, and strengthened.

For all of these reasons, Opposing Viewpoints continues to be exactly the right resource at exactly the right time—when we most need to provide readers with the critical-thinking tools and skills that will not only serve them well in school but also in their careers and their daily lives as decision-making family members, community members, and citizens. This series encourages respectful engagement with and analysis of opposing viewpoints and fosters a resulting increase in the strength and rigor of one's own opinions and stances. As such, it helps make readers "future ready," and that readiness will pay rich dividends for the readers themselves, for the citizenry, for our society, and for the world at large.

Introduction

"The test of our progress is not whether we add more to the abundance of those who have much; it is whether we provide enough for those who have too little."

> —*Franklin D. Roosevelt,*
> *Inaugural Address,*
> *January 20, 1937*

In 1938, in the midst of the Great Depression, the United States Congress passed the Fair Labor Standards Act (FLSA). The FLSA established some basic standards for employment in the United States. In addition to child labor laws, overtime pay, and record-keeping regulations, the legislation established a minimum wage of twenty-five cents an hour. (Since then, some states have implemented their own minimum wages. In Wyoming and Georgia, where the state minimum wage is lower than the federal, the federal rate takes precedence over the local.)

Since 1938, the federal minimum wage has been raised periodically, twenty-two times in all. The most recent increase (as of this writing) was in 2009, when it was raised to $7.25 an hour. However, in the 1980s, a belief in the power of free markets and a fear that raising wages would harm businesses brought an end to those semi-regular wage boosts.

As the wage increases virtually stopped, poverty and income inequality has grown. According to Pew Research, in 1980 top households had incomes roughly nine times the incomes of those at the bottom. And that gap has only grown over the last three decades. In 2018, the difference was 12.6. That's an increase of almost 40 percent in three decades.

And many of those at the bottom work full-time jobs. As of 2019, the most recent year for which data is available, 37 percent of American households do not make enough money to pay for the basics—housing, food, utilities—in their neighborhoods, according to a report by the Brookings Institution. Forty-seven percent of Black households and 50 percent of Hispanic households have difficulty making ends meet. How much it takes to pay the basic bills varies from city to city. The report looked at fifty-three metro areas and found that it typically took $14.70 per hour just to get by. Yet the federal minimum wage is less than half that. Not only is poverty growing in America, many of the poor work full-time jobs.

Fight for Fifteen

In November 2012, two hundred fast-food workers walked off their jobs to protest low pay. Soon underpaid workers in many cities and in a variety of industries joined the walkout. The protest quickly became a movement called "The Fight for Fifteen," demanding a minimum wage of $15—enough to get by in most parts of the country. At first, the "Fight for Fifteen" focused its attention mostly at the local level, and it has had some successes. By 2021, twenty states and many cities had increased their minimum wages, making them higher than the federal minimum. Some places, such as Seattle, made it all the way to $15. Now the fight has turned to the national level. It's time, organizers say, for Congress to make a $15 minimum wage the law of the land.

It may seem like a no-brainer. People who work full-time should be able to support themselves and their families. However, many businesses (small and large) say that paying a $15 minimum wage (even if it is phased in gradually, which is what most proposals suggest) would be a serious hardship forcing them to fire workers in order to stay in business. An increased minimum wage would, they argue, actually make things worse for workers. This is not a new argument. In 1980, then president Ronald Reagan said, "The minimum wage has caused more misery and unemployment than anything since the Great Depression." This was obviously hyperbole. Nonetheless, a steep and sudden increase might, according to some non-partisan economists, lead to some job losses.

Meanwhile, other non-partisan economists argue that an increase would not lead to job losses. When workers have more money to spend, businesses will make greater profits, causing them to need to hire even more workers.

In chapters titled "Will Raising the Minimum Wage Reduce Poverty?" "Is Raising the Minimum Wage Unfair to Workers?" "Would Raising the Minimum Wage Harm Businesses?" and "Is Raising the Minimum Wage a Moral Imperative?," viewpoint authors explore many facets of this issue. The progression of diverse perspectives reveals that the economics of an increased minimum wage can be complicated and uncertain. The moral question may be complex as well. However, the question of how much businesses should be obligated to pay their workers is one of the most important issues of our day.

OPPOSING
VIEWPOINTS®
SERIES

CHAPTER 1

Will Raising the Minimum Wage Reduce Poverty?

Chapter Preface

One of the most basic and most common justifications for increasing the minimum wage is that doing so would reduce poverty. It seems obvious: pay low-wage workers enough to live on and fewer people will be poor. However, many experts argue that it's not as simple as that. A mandated minimum wage would have ripple effects on the economy, and determining exactly what those effects might be is not straightforward. In addition, both the cost of living and the cost of doing business varies from state to state and even from city to city. Clearly, paying people more will help many individuals and families. However, if it reduces the number of jobs available to low-wage workers, the end result may not be beneficial for everyone.

In this chapter, the viewpoint authors examine the issue of the effect that a substantially increased minimum wage has on poverty. Some point to data showing millions of workers and their children would be lifted from poverty if the minimum wage were increased to $15 per hour. Others see more nuance in the numbers and claim that the end result would not in fact reduce the burden of poverty overall.

The first viewpoint takes a local perspective, looking at the effect of an increased minimum on workers in small and mid-sized cities. Then we hear from authors who point out that businesses—particularly fast-food restaurants—will likely respond by raising prices. This means that customers will pay for the increased labor costs. When the customers are themselves low-wage earners, they will in effect be helping pay for their own raises. Other authors point out that the market will bear only so much price increases and that businesses have other ways to offset increased labor costs. Higher pay will offset the increased prices for individuals. Other writers add that if the cost is spread out among society, so are the benefits. If all workers make a living wage, taxpayers will spend less on food and housing assistance to the poor. This will free up money for other beneficial programs.

> "Households in small metro areas,
> micropolitan areas, and rural
> areas are more likely to reach
> self-sufficiency with a $15 federal
> minimum wage."

A $15 Minimum Wage Would Help Millions of Struggling Households

Joseph Parilla and Sifan Liu

In the following viewpoint, Joseph Parilla and Sifan Liu argue that increasing the minimum wage could help millions of households achieve self-sufficiency. The authors go on to explore the variations in location and family composition that affect the impact a higher wage floor would make. In many small and mid-sized cities, an increased minimum wage would help millions of households become self-sufficient. Joseph Parilla is a fellow at the Brookings Metropolitan Policy Program, where Sifan Liu is a senior research analyst.

As you read, consider the following questions:

1. What are two advantages of increasing the minimum wage?
2. How does family composition impact self-sufficiency?
3. Why do local economies matter in minimum wage discussions?

"A $15 Minimum Wage Would Help Millions of Struggling Households in Small and Mid-Sized Cities Achieve Self-Sufficiency," March 17, 2021. This post was originally published on brookings.edu by Joseph Parilla and Sifan Liu.

On March 11, President Joe Biden signed the $1.9 trillion American Rescue Plan into law. But an earlier, House-passed provision to increase the federal minimum wage to $15 per hour was not included.

According to the Congressional Budget Office, the $15 federal minimum wage would have boosted the earnings of low-wage workers and decreased poverty. In its absence, a national policy agenda focused on raising wages is still urgently needed.

For now, at least, increasing the minimum wage will remain a bottom-up exercise led by local and state policymakers. In a new report, we argue that raising the wage floor can not only help reduce poverty (a worthy goal unto itself), but it can also support individual and family self-sufficiency—the ability to cover living expenses without relying on public subsidies.

To understand the landscape of struggling individuals and households, our report asked a simple question: Do individuals and families earn enough to make ends meet in the communities where they live?

We found that for a large share of the US population, wages leave them short of self-sufficiency. As of 2019 (the latest data available), 37% of US households—38 million overall—did not earn a pre-tax, pre-transfer wage that allowed them to make ends meet, including 14 million households with children. Owing to historical racial injustices and structural inequities, 47% of Black households and 50% of Latino or Hispanic households struggle to make ends meet.

A local perspective here is critical, because the share of households that struggle to make ends meet varies considerably across the United States due to diverging labor market conditions and costs of living. Over 40% of households were struggling to make ends meet in places such as Miami, Las Vegas, Orlando, Fla., and Los Angeles. In contrast, the struggling share of households was closer to 25% for Pittsburgh, Boston, and Seattle.

To understand more precisely how the minimum wage or other policies might alleviate these challenges, we estimate a "family-sustaining wage" threshold for each metro area that would help lift half of its struggling households into self-sufficiency. Looking at all households, including those without children, family-sustaining wage thresholds range from $12 in Brownsville, Texas, to $23 in San Jose, Calif. Among 53 metro areas with at least 1 million residents, the typical family-sustaining wage threshold is around $14.70 per hour—close to the value for regions such as Nashville, Tenn., and Birmingham, Ala.

While wages and living expenses differ, every metro area has more struggling individuals and families than jobs that pay family-sustaining wages. Our data interactive lists these figures for 192 US metro areas, and suggests that higher wage floors will not only reduce poverty and improve earnings for low-wage workers, but they also can make a meaningful difference in economic self-sufficiency—especially for households without children.

Indeed, a key finding of our analysis is that the impact of a higher minimum wage on family self-sufficiency depends greatly on family composition. Consider a thought experiment in which the entire nation adopts a $15 minimum wage. Single-adult households account for 19 million of the nation's struggling households—about half of such households—yet they represent more than three-quarters of households that could reach self-sufficiency with a $15 wage. On the other hand, 14 million—or 40%—of all struggling households are families with children, but they account for only 14% of households that would reach self-sufficiency with a $15 wage.

The geographic variation is even more striking. Because the cost of living is substantially lower in smaller communities, households in small metro areas, micropolitan areas, and rural areas are more likely to reach self-sufficiency with a $15 federal minimum wage. Among the struggling households that would make ends meet with a $15 minimum wage, only 45% are in very large metro areas with populations exceeding 1 million—smaller than the 57% of struggling households they account for.

Significant variations exist even within those large and very large metro areas. In the nation's most expensive places—San Jose, Calif., San Francisco, Honolulu, Washington, D.C., and New York—fewer than 10% of struggling households would achieve self-sufficiency with a $15 hourly wage. Many of these cities and their states have already enacted policies to increase their minimum wages. In comparison, more than two-thirds of struggling households in Madison, Wis., Lansing, Mich., and Pittsburgh would achieve self-sufficiency with a $15 hourly wage. Many of these metro areas contain large universities and likely reflect the significant number of student households living (temporarily) on low wages.

One strand of the debate about raising the federal minimum wage has registered concerns about disparate regional impacts—particularly, that a $15 minimum wage would prove too costly for businesses in low-cost regional economies. But viewed from the perspective of workers and families, it is in those same smaller, more affordable cities where a higher minimum wage could lift the largest shares of struggling families into self-sufficiency. Notably, in many metro areas (including some large metro areas), a wage threshold set between $12 and $13 per hour would lift half of struggling households—a majority of whom are childless households—into self-sufficiency.

In the end, economic self-sufficiency—whether households can make ends meet through their wage income alone—is just one metric for assessing the efficacy of policies like a minimum wage increase. But for the tens of millions of Americans struggling to afford the costs of living in their local communities, it's arguably the metric that matters most.

> *"The increase in their 'real wage'—that is, their wage after accounting for the price of the stuff they buy—is not as high, because the cost of some of the stuff they buy, such as fast food, goes up too."*

Workers May End Up Paying for Part of Their Increased Minimum Wage

Greg Rosalsky

In the following viewpoint, Greg Rosalsky speaks with economists who study the minimum wage's impact on the economy by looking closely at the McDonald's restaurant company, the largest fast-food chain in the world. These economists found that while an increase in wages at McDonald's is important and beneficial to workers, the actual increase in income is not as great as it seems. This is because the company recoups the cost of paying higher wages by increasing the price of its food. Because minimum wage workers are often also McDonald's customers, they end up paying for part of their own wage increases. Still, the increase seemed beneficial overall. Greg Rosalsky is an economics reporter for National Public Radio.

As you read, consider the following questions:

1. Why is McDonald's the perfect laboratory for studying different labor markets, according to sources cited in the viewpoint?
2. Why, according to the author, might companies like McDonald's want to offer wages slightly above minimum wage?
3. Why might minimum wage increases at places like McDonald's not mean as big a raise for employees as one would expect?

O n Nov. 29, 2012, dozens of fast-food workers assembled at a McDonald's in Midtown Manhattan to demand better pay. Their demonstration kicked off a massive wave of protests for a $15 minimum wage. Since then, cities and states around the US have taken action. And now, the federal government, led by President Biden and a Democratic-controlled Congress, has begun to consider making the $15 minimum wage national.

McDonald's is one of the nation's biggest employers of low-wage workers. As such, it was kind of the perfect place to launch what was, in retrospect, the beginning of a historic labor movement. A new study by economists Orley Ashenfelter and Štěpán Jurajda suggests McDonald's is also kind of the perfect place to test the effects of the minimum wage increases that workers have been fighting for.

Ashenfelter is an economist at Princeton University, and he has spent a couple of decades studying McDonald's. Back in 2012, when he was president of the American Economic Association, he even dedicated part of his big presidential address to the company. And it wasn't just because, as he told us, his "favorite meal is fries, a chocolate shake and a Big Mac." He views McDonald's as a kind of natural "laboratory" to compare and contrast different labor markets. I mean, think about it: Each McDonald's restaurant is pretty much the same. The workers have almost identical jobs, regardless of which part of the world they're in; the food they make is generally the same; and McDonald's restaurants are basically everywhere.

Meanwhile, over the last decade, a McFlurry of cities and states has been raising their minimum wages. In their new study, Ashenfelter and Jurajda use McDonald's restaurants as kind of like treatment and control groups to assess the impact of these new minimum wage laws. They obtained data on hourly wage rates of McDonald's "Basic Crew" employees, the prices of Big Macs and other information from about 10,000 McDonald's restaurants between 2016 and 2020. And they crunched the numbers to see what happens when a city or state increases its minimum wage.

One big fear of a higher minimum wage is that it could cause businesses to replace their workers with machines. Ashenfelter and Jurajda found that some McDonald's restaurants have already installed touch screens so customers can input their meal orders without interacting with a human being. But they also found that those touch screens weren't installed in response to higher minimum wages. "We couldn't find any relationship between minimum wage increases and the adoption of touch-screen technology," Ashenfelter says.

Not surprisingly, Ashenfelter and Jurajda found that McDonald's restaurants raise their wages after a city or state raises its minimum wage. More surprisingly, they found that a substantial fraction of restaurants preserve their pay premiums for workers who were previously earning more than the minimum wage. That is, if a worker was making a dollar more than the old minimum wage, many McDonald's will make sure those workers continue to make a dollar more than the new minimum wage. Ashenfelter says they don't have hard evidence for why this is, but he believes it's because certain restaurants want to offer wages slightly higher than the legal minimum as a way to reduce turnover. Paying above the minimum wage creates a kind of magnet for workers. Overall, the economists found that if the minimum wage goes up by 10%,

SMALL, PHASED-IN MINIMUM WAGE HIKES MAY ACTUALLY REDUCE PRICES

Many business leaders fear that any increase in the minimum wage will be passed on to consumers through price increases thereby slowing spending and economic growth, but that may not be the case. New research shows that the pass-through effect on prices is fleeting and much smaller than previously thought.

In a new Upjohn Institute working paper, Daniel MacDonald and Eric Nilsson, of California State University, Bernardino, advance the literature on price effects of minimum wage increases.

Historically, minimum wage increases were large, one-shot changes imposed with little advance notice for businesses. But many recent state and city-level minimum wage increases have been scheduled to be implemented over time and often are indexed to some measure of price inflation. These small, scheduled minimum wage hikes seem to have smaller effects on prices than large, one-time increases.

By looking at changes in restaurant food pricing during the period of 1978–2015, MacDonald and Nilsson find that prices rose by just 0.36 percent for every 10 percent increase in the minimum wage, which is only about half the size reported in previous studies. They also observe that small minimum wage increases do not lead to higher prices and may actually reduce prices. Furthermore, it is also possible that small minimum wage increases could lead to increased employment in low-wage labor markets.

While federal and state minimum wage increases appear to produce similar results, more research is needed to fully grasp the effects of city minimum-wage raises.

"Does Increasing the Minimum Wage Lead to Higher Prices?" UpJohn.

the average McDonald's restaurant will increase worker wages by about 7%.

Finally and perhaps most thought provokingly, the economists looked at the effects of minimum wage hikes on the prices of Big Macs. They found that when the minimum wage goes up, the price of a Big Mac goes up too. Ashenfelter says the evidence from increased food prices suggests that basically all of the "increase of labor costs gets passed right on to the customers." But because low-wage workers are also usually customers at low-wage establishments, this suggests that any pay raise resulting from a minimum wage increase might not be as great in reality as it looks on paper. In econospeak, the increase in their "real wage"—that is, their wage after accounting for the price of the stuff they buy—is not as high, because the cost of some of the stuff they buy, such as fast food, goes up too.

However, Ashenfelter says, the fast-food workers they studied were still, on the net, much better off. "They still get a raise. They just don't get as big a raise as it may seem," he says. In effect, a minimum wage increase appears to be a redistribution of wealth from customers to low-wage workers. Ashenfelter says he thinks of it like a kind of sales tax. And for whatever reason, unlike with many other types of taxes, the minimum wage tax seems to be more popular with voters—even in many red states, like Florida, where they're voting to increase the minimum wage.

The one big disappointment from Ashenfelter and Jurajda's study is they're unable to tell us much about the effects of minimum wages on employment, which is at the center of the debate about the policy. They couldn't obtain data on hiring and firing from McDonald's restaurants around the nation.

It's worth remembering that McDonald's was also at the center of the famous study by David Card and Alan Krueger that revolutionized economic thinking about the minimum wage. Card and Krueger found no evidence that New Jersey's hike of the minimum wage from $4.25 to $5.05 an hour reduced employment at fast-food restaurants there. Would the same happen in the entire nation if the federal government raised it from $7.25 to $15? Last week, the Congressional Budget Office, while saying a $15 minimum wage would reduce poverty, cast doubt on the idea that there would be no substantial job losses.

> *"The bump from $290 a week to $600 a week would lift millions of families out of poverty."*

Increasing the Minimum Wage Would Fix Many Problems

Mary Babic

In the following viewpoint, Mary Babic outlines six reasons the US government should raise the federal minimum wage. She argues that the people doing minimum wage work are crucial to the economy and society. Raising the federal minimum wage would lift millions out of poverty while also reducing racial and gender inequality and the amount taxpayers spend on government programs. Mary Babic is senior communications officer for the domestic program at Oxfam America.

As you read, consider the following questions:

1. How would increasing the minimum wage help reduce racial and gender inequalities, according to the author?
2. How would increasing the minimum wage reduce the amount taxpayers spend on federal programs?
3. Why do many small business owners support an increase in the minimum wage?

"6 Simple Reasons We Should Raise the Minimum Wage Right Now," by Mary Babic, Oxfam, February 5, 2021. Reprinted by permission.

It's time to raise the minimum wage. Today, millions of Americans do arduous work in jobs that pay too little and offer too few benefits. They serve food, clean offices, care for the young and elderly, stock shelves, and deliver pizza. They work these jobs year after year while caring for children and parents, trying to save for college, and paying their bills.

But despite their best efforts, these low-wage and essential workers are falling further and further behind. The COVID-19 crisis has put them even more at risk, and the federal minimum wage of $7.25/hr is locking millions—most notably women of color and single parents—in poverty.

The way we see it, if you work hard, you should earn enough to get by. That's why new efforts by the Biden administration and Congress to raise the federal minimum wage to $15 to help Americans recover from COVID-19 are so important.

Here are six simple reasons why raising the minimum wage makes sense.

1. It Is Long Overdue

Since it was last raised in 2009, the minimum wage has failed to keep up with inflation, failed to keep up with average wages, and—most dramatically—failed to keep up with incomes of the top 1 percent and CEOs, contributing to America's growing inequality crisis.

As a result, low-wage workers are not benefiting from economic growth and productivity. If the minimum wage had kept pace with productivity increases, it would be around $24/hr according to the Center for Economic and Policy Research. Just 30 years ago, the average pay gap between CEOs and workers was 59 to 1; by 2018, it had soared to 361 to 1. The average CEO at one of the top 350 firms in the US made $21.3 million in 2019, 320 times as much as the typical worker; a minimum wage worker still makes $15,080: a gap of 1,400 to 1.

2. It Would Address Longstanding Racial and Gender Inequities

Historically marginalized people, who do more than their fair share of low-wage work, would stand to benefit disproportionately from the bump.

According to the data from the Economic Policy Institute, while 27 percent of the total US workforce would benefit from the raise:

- 39 percent of Black and Latina women would benefit (vs. 18 percent of white men);
- 38 percent of African American workers would benefit;
- 33 percent of Latino workers would benefit; and
- 32 percent of women workers would benefit (vs. 22 percent of men).

3. It Would Reduce Poverty

The bump from $290 a week to $600 a week would lift millions of families out of poverty. More than a quarter of the workforce—40 million workers—would see a raise in wages.

The pandemic has made this move even more urgent, as millions have slipped into poverty over the past year, and 11 percent of adults are now facing food insecurity.

4. It Would Fuel Economic Growth

The roughly $120 billion extra paid to workers would be pumped back into the economy for necessities such as rent, food, and clothes. Economists have long recognized that boosting purchasing power by putting money in people's pockets for consumer spending has positive ripple effects on the entire economy.

In one recent poll, 67 percent of small business owners support the minimum wage increase to $15 an hour. They say it would spark consumer demand, which would enable them to retain or hire new employees.

And raising the wage doesn't seem to compel employers to cut jobs. As states and cities across the country have raised wages, research has found no statistically significant effect on employment.

5. It Would Save Taxpayer Money and Reduce Use of Government Programs

When employers don't pay people enough to survive, those workers are compelled to seek government assistance, meaning taxpayers are essentially subsidizing the corporations.

In 2016, the Economic Policy Institute found that, among recipients of public assistance, most work or have a family member who works; and they are concentrated at the bottom of the pay scale. Raising wages for low-wage workers would "unambiguously reduce net spending on public assistance, particularly among workers likely to be affected by a federal minimum-wage increase."

6. It's What the Vast Majority of Americans Want

Vast majorities (up to three quarters, including a majority across party lines) support raising the wage. In fact, over half the states have raised their minimum wages to restore basic fairness to the workforce.

All work has dignity and worth. We need to get our economy moving, prioritizing workers and families most impacted by the pandemic, specifically women and people of color. After more than a decade of hard work, low-wage workers deserve a bump to get them and their families out of poverty.

> *"Large minimum-wage increases require large price increases. The burden of these price increases falls disproportionately on low-income and middle-income Americans."*

$15 Minimum Wages Will Substantially Raise Prices and Burden the Poor

James Sherk

A previous article pointed out that some of the cost of minimum wage increases might be borne by the very people the increases are meant to benefit. However, that viewpoint found that the increase was still a net benefit. In the following excerpted viewpoint, James Sherk argues that when employers pass on to customers the cost of paying higher wages, the benefit of wage increases will be lost. James Sherk is director of the Center for American Freedom at the America First Policy Institute.

As you read, consider the following questions:

1. How do businesses respond to minimum wage mandates?
2. Why would minimum wage increases affect southern companies more than northern ones?
3. How much does a 10 percent increase in starting wages increase the price of a hamburger?

"$15 Minimum Wages Will Substantially Raise Prices," by James Sherk, The Heritage Foundation, January 19, 2017. Reprinted by permission.

Many Americans believe that minimum-wage increases transfer income from business owners to their workers. This impression is incorrect. Most firms employing minimum-wage workers are relatively small businesses, such as fast-food restaurants or "Mom and Pop" retail stores.[1] These firms typically operate in highly competitive markets. As a result, they have fairly low profit margins. The typical fast-food restaurant, for example, earns between 3 cents and 6 cents of profit on each dollar of sales.[2] Most minimum-wage employers could not take the entire cost of higher wages out of their profits, even if they wanted to. And if their profit margins fell significantly, many of these small business owners would seek different lines of work. When starting wages rise, these businesses pass the cost on to their customers and employees.

Most discussion of minimum-wage increases focuses on the employees: Some receive higher pay—at the cost of others being forced to work fewer hours, or being let go.[3] Relatively little attention is paid to how minimum-wage increases affect prices. But customers provide the revenues that cover business expenses. When costs rise, businesses generally compensate by raising prices. Minimum-wage increases are no exception.

Of course, most firms cannot raise prices by themselves without losing business to competitors. A unilateral increase in McDonald's burger prices would send diners to Burger King or Wendy's. But when cost increases hit every firm in an industry, these firms can collectively raise prices. Though higher prices will drive some customers away, no single firm faces a competitive disadvantage.

As a result, most affected businesses respond to mandatory starting-wage increases by raising prices. As the federal Minimum Wage Study Commission found, "The most common types of [employer] responses to the increase in the minimum wage were price increases and wage ripples. No single type of disemployment response was reported with nearly the frequency of these."[4] Customers, not business owners, pay for minimum-wage increases.

Research: Prices Rise

Economists have not studied the minimum wage's price effects as extensively as its employment effects. But the research they have conducted points to higher prices.

Sarah Lemos of the University of Leicester surveyed roughly 30 studies conducted before 2005 examining minimum-wage price effects.[5] These studies found that minimum-wage increases have relatively small effects on the overall price level. They reported that a 10 percent minimum-wage increase raises overall prices by about 0.2 percent to 0.3 percent. Most businesses pay more than the current minimum wage, so minimum-wage increases do not affect their costs or prices very much. But Lemos found that studies of industries with higher concentrations of minimum-wage workers generally showed larger price effects.

One noteworthy study that Lemos surveyed examined the federal minimum wage in the 1970s.[6] The federal minimum wage affects Southern businesses more than Northern firms.[7] Southern states have lower living costs and lower wages than the rest of the US; these differences were even greater in the 1970s than today. The study found the South's higher effective minimum wage increased service prices. Each 10 percent difference in the effective minimum wage raised Southern service prices by 2.7 percent. It had no effect on the prices of manufactured goods.

This finding fits with economic theory. Southern manufacturers compete nationally and internationally. Higher effective Southern minimum wages do not affect their competitors in other states or countries. Affected manufacturers cannot raise prices without losing customers. However, services are local. Restaurants and hotels paying higher wages compete with local companies whose costs have also risen. Such companies can, and do, respond by raising prices.

More recent research comes to the same conclusion as the studies Lemos surveyed. Daniel Aaronson, Eric French, and James MacDonald, researchers at the Federal Reserve Bank of Chicago and the Department of Agriculture, published a study in 2008 examining how restaurants respond to minimum-wage increases.[8] They used Consumer Price Index (CPI) data and examined the 1996–1997 federal minimum-wage increase. They found that a 10 percent increase in the minimum wage raises overall restaurant prices approximately 0.7 percent. Unsurprisingly, they found larger effects in restaurants that employ more minimum-wage workers. Prices increased twice as much—by approximately 1.5 percent—at fast-food restaurants. In lower-wage regions, fast-food prices rose 1.8 percent. Aaronson, French, and MacDonald concluded that their results are consistent with restaurants passing the full cost of minimum-wage increases on to customers, although their results were too imprecise to ascertain whether this actually occurred.

In 2010, Denis Fougère, Erwan Gautier, and Hervé Le Bihan, researchers at the Bank of France, criticized the econometric model that Aaronson and his co-authors used.[9] They concluded that that model inaccurately estimates minimum-wage price effects.[10] They used data from the French version of the CPI and examined how France's annual minimum-wage increases affect restaurant prices. They concluded that a 10 percent minimum-wage increase raises restaurant prices by approximately 1 percent, although it takes one to three years for price increases to fully materialize.[11]

Their estimate was higher than that found by Aaronson and his coauthors. That difference may result from Fougère and his colleagues using a better methodology; it could also occur because France has a higher minimum wage than the United States. Consequently, French minimum-wage increases have a greater effect on restaurant costs. Fougère and his coauthors found somewhat less than full-cost pass-through, but they could not rule out the possibility that French restaurants passed on the entire cost of minimum-wage increases to their customers.[12]

One exception to the general finding that restaurants pass almost all minimum-wage cost increases directly to customers comes from Daniel MacDonald and Eric Nilsson, two researchers from California State University at San Bernardino.[13] They found that consumers bear only half the cost of minimum-wage increases through higher prices. However, these researchers used a similar approach to Aaronson and his coauthors. Fougère and his colleagues also found less than full-cost pass-through in their French data when they used that econometric model.[14] Most other studies have found that businesses pass either the vast majority, or all, of the costs of starting-wage increases to their customers.

Even left-leaning researchers come to this conclusion. Sylvia Allegretto and Michael Reich are economists at the University of California at Berkeley. Both publicly advocate raising the minimum wage. These researchers examined how San Jose's 2013 starting-wage increase (to $10 an hour) affected restaurant prices.[15] Using online menu data, they concluded that San Jose restaurants passed essentially the full-wage increase on to their customers.

Emek Basker and Muhammad Khan, researchers at the Census Bureau and the Islamic Development Bank, respectively, came to a similar conclusion in 2016.[16] These researchers used data from a community survey used to estimate cost-of-living differences between cities.[17] This survey records the price of a McDonald's quarter-pounder, a regular Pizza Hut cheese pizza, and Kentucky Fried Chicken fried drumsticks across America. They found that a 10 percent increase in required starting wages raises the price of burgers and pizza by about 1 percent. Curiously they found little effect on KFC chicken prices.[18] They report that their findings are consistent with full pass-through of costs to consumers—if payrolls account for half of fast-food restaurants' costs.

Interestingly, most data show that fast-food restaurants spend only a quarter of their budget on wages and benefits.[19] Basker and Khan's findings thus suggest that restaurants may raise prices more than what is necessary to cover costs.

[…]

Higher Prices Negate Anti-Poverty Effects

Consumers pay for higher minimum wages through higher prices. Large minimum-wage increases require large price increases. The burden of these price increases falls disproportionately on low-income and middle-income Americans. These price increases are more regressive than sales taxes.

This dynamic largely negates minimum-wage increases' anti-poverty effects. Everyone in society—not just business owners—pays the costs through higher prices. Meanwhile, the benefits go to families up and down the income distribution. On balance, minimum-wage increases provide little net benefit to the poor; in fact, more low-income families lose than gain. Minimum-wage increases do not accomplish what their supporters claim they will.

Endnotes

1. Over three-fifths of workers who receive the federal minimum wage work in two economic sectors: "retail trade" or "leisure and hospitality" (which includes restaurants). Note: A substantially larger share of workers earning "below the minimum wage" work in the leisure and hospitality sector than workers who are paid exactly the minimum wage. This is because federal law allows restaurants to pay hourly rates below the minimum wage, provided their employees earn more than the minimum wage after tips. However, the survey used to construct these tables does not include tips in its definition of hourly wages. Consequently, many restaurant employees appear to make less than the minimum wage, even though their actual income may be substantially higher after taking tips into account.

2. IBISWorld, "Industry Report 72221a: Fast Food Restaurants in the US," May 2013, and National Restaurant Association, Restaurant Operations Report: 2013–2014 Edition, p. 102.

3. See, for example, Jeffrey Clemens and Michael Wither, "The Minimum Wage and the Great Recession: Evidence of Effects on the Employment and Income Trajectories of Low-Skilled Workers," University of California at San Diego, November 24, 2014, http://econweb.ucsd.edu/~mwither/pdfs/Effects%20of%20Min%20Wage%20on%20 Wages%20Employment%20and%20Earnings.pdf (accessed September 9, 2016).

4. Muriel Converse et al., "The Minimum Wage: An Employer Survey," in Report of the Minimum Wage Commission (Washington DC: US Government Printing Office, 1981), pp. 241–341.

5. Sara Lemos, "A Survey of the Effects of the Minimum Wage on Prices," *Journal of Economic Surveys*, Vol. 22, No. 1 (2008), pp. 187–212.

6. Walter Wessels, *Minimum Wages, Fringe Benefits and Working Conditions* (Washington, DC: American Enterprise Institute, 1980).

7. In 1979, the federal minimum wage covered about one-tenth of workers in Massachusetts, New Jersey, and New York. It covered approximately one-fifth of workers in Alabama, Arkansas, and Mississippi. Author's analysis using data from the 1979 Current Population Survey Outgoing Rotation Groups.

8. Daniel Aaronson, Eric French, and James MacDonald, "The Minimum Wage, Restaurant Prices, and Labor Market Structure," *The Journal of Human Resources*, Vol. 43, No. 3 (Summer 2008), pp. 688–720.

Poverty, Prosperity, and the Minimum Wage

9. Denis Fougère, Erwan Gautier, and Hervé Le Bihan, "Restaurant Prices and the Minimum Wage," *Journal of Money, Credit, and Banking,* Vol. 42, No. 7 (October 2010), pp. 1199–1234.

10. They conduct Monte Carlo simulations and show that a linear model with distributed lags and an aggregate price index will asymptotically converge to the true value of price pass-through. However, the speed of this convergence is slow and in "small" samples (that is, the sizes currently available to researchers) this model will systematically overstate the speed of price adjustment. Moreover, a linear distributed lag model with aggregate price data produces very high standard deviations across simulations in small samples (on the order of twice the true-effect size in the data-generating process); results using this model are estimated very imprecisely.

11. More precisely, they found an increase of approximately 1 percent for traditional sit-down restaurants and 1.2 percent for fast-food restaurants. See Fougère, Gautier, and Le Bihan, "Restaurant Prices and the Minimum Wage," p. 1227.

12. Their confidence interval on their estimates included values consistent with full cost pass-through.

13. Daniel MacDonald and Eric Nilsson, "The Effects of Increasing the Minimum Wage on Prices: Analyzing the Incidence of Policy Design and Context," Upjohn Institute Working Paper 16-260, 2016.

14. Fougère, Gautier, and Le Bihan, "Restaurant Prices and the Minimum Wage," Table 2. Full pass-through in their data corresponded to a long-run elasticity of 0.15. They estimated elasticities ranging between 0.012 and 0.148 when they used aggregated price data and a linear distributed lags model, with the exact coefficient highly sensitive to choice of control variables. A related concern is that Fougère, Gautier, and Le Bihan found that prices take one to three years to fully adjust to price increases. MacDonald and Nilsson only looked at a four-month window surrounding minimum-wage hikes, so they may have missed part of the total effect.

15. Sylvia Allegretto and Michael Reich, "Are Local Minimum Wages Absorbed by Price Increases?" Institute for Research on Labor and Employment Working Paper No. 125-15, December 2015.

16. Emek Basker and Muhammad Taimur Khan, "Does the Minimum Wage Bite into Fast-Food Prices?" *Journal of Labor Research,* Vol. 37 (2016), pp. 129–148.

17. Council for Community and Economic Research, "Cost of Living Index," https://www .coli.org/ (accessed September 8, 2016).

18. Allegretto and Reich examined menu price responses for hamburger, pizza, and chicken dishes separately. They found somewhat smaller price increases for these goods than for the entire universe of menu items they examined.

19. Basker and Khan (2016) present data showing labor expenses are almost half of sales revenue in the fast-food sector. This is at odds with almost all other data sources on this topic. For example, the Census Bureau's 2012 Economic Census reported that "limited-service restaurants" (aka fast food) had payrolls of $45.4 billion on sales of $185.4 billion in 2012. Payrolls thus represent 24.5 percent of their total revenues. See also IBISWorld, "Industry Report 72221a: Fast Food Restaurants in the US," May 2013, which reports payrolls account for 26 percent of fast-food restaurants' total revenues.

| 38

> "Restaurants with good reviews were much less likely to go out of business. This suggests well-operated, customer-focused restaurants will retain diners and stay in business."

Well-Run Restaurants Will Adapt to Minimum Wage Increases

Michael von Massow

We've seen viewpoints claiming that increasing the minimum wage will increase prices in chain restaurants. In the following viewpoint, Michael von Massow goes into some detail about how such increases might and might not affect the restaurant industry. The author argues that price increases are limited by what customers are willing to spend. Too much of a rise, and restaurants will lose business. On the other hand, Massow suggests, customers might notice smaller portions and reduced hours as restaurants try to protect profit margins. Michael von Massow is associate professor of food economics at the University of Guelph.

"Higher Prices, Reduced Hours: Restaurants and Minimum Wage Hikes," by Michael von Massow, The Conversation, January 7, 2018. https://theconversation.com/higher -prices-reduced-hours-restaurants-and-minimum-wage-hikes-89487. Licensed under CC BY-ND-4.0 International.

As you read, consider the following questions:

1. What other cost pressures on restaurants in some areas does von Massow mention?
2. What options besides increasing prices to restaurants have to protect profit margins?
3. According to the viewpoint, what types of restaurants are most likely to survive mandated wage increases?

There is considerable concern in the restaurant industry about minimum wage hikes. A higher minimum wage poses significant challenges for restaurants, although well-run operations should find ways to adapt.

Canada's iconic and highly profitable chain Tim Hortons, as well as other restaurants, have already found themselves at the centre of a storm in Ontario for what they say are minimum-wage related cuts.

Ontario's minimum wage increased on Jan. 1, with further increases coming. Alberta has increased its minimum wage and so have several American jurisdictions. British Columbia has also signalled that increases are coming.

Adapting to the change will be hard for some restaurants. The cost increase will be significant, and the short timeline has not given restaurants much time to prepare.

Most restaurants are not high-margin businesses, so something will have to give. Restaurants Canada, in fact, reports that average profit margins in Canadian restaurants are less than five per cent. That doesn't leave a lot of room for higher labour costs.

There are studies suggesting that higher minimum wages don't lead to lower employment. I've also seen some anecdotal discussion of specific markets such as Seattle in which a higher minimum wage hasn't hurt restaurant jobs growth at all a year after it was implemented.

Understanding the dynamics of individual markets is always difficult. There are so many factors at play that it's difficult to attribute change to a specific measure.

Regardless, increased labour costs will require changes at restaurants. Here are some that are likely in store:

Prices Increase, Portion Sizes Decrease

Prices will inevitably go up. There are likely some things that restaurants can do to trim costs, but I suspect that many of these measures have already been taken given food prices have been rising in the past few years.

In some markets, particularly Toronto, escalating rents have also put pressure on restaurants.

But price increases will have to be executed strategically. A 10 per cent, across-the-board hike would be unlikely to yield a 10 per cent increase in how much the average diner spends. People might cut back on appetizers, desserts or drinks in response. And so making price changes strategic is critical for restaurants.

If prices are hiked too much, it could cause people to eat out less, reducing overall demand due to fewer outings.

Portion sizes may change. The pour of a glass of wine might be less generous. The size of the salmon filet could be skimpier.

Reducing costs could be an alternative to increasing prices. But as mentioned, that's largely already happened. Restaurants also need to be careful to continue to meet consumer value expectations. No one wants to go to a restaurant to be served a tiny portion of a mediocre cut of meat.

Menus will change. Less profitable or more exotic items that aren't ordered often will be removed. We will likely see more non-traditional cuts of meat, less beef and perhaps more vegetarian options, or items with smaller meat portions or with less emphasis on the meat element of a dish.

A demand for plant-based proteins is expected to increase in coming years, and this change in restaurant menus could accelerate the trend to replace or supplement meat proteins.

Operational Changes May Result

Restaurants may restrict hours. Many restaurants are open on days of the week, or during parts of the day, that simply don't attract a lot of customers and are therefore unprofitable. Staffing these down times will become more expensive, and will likely lead to the decision to reduce hours.

This should probably have already been happening, but the wage increase will likely accelerate it.

It will result in either fewer jobs or, more likely, fewer hours for those working at restaurants. That would mean staff earn more per hour, but their take-home pay won't increase because they're working fewer hours—meaning that, for some, the minimum wage increase won't mean much to their take-home pay.

Restaurants may rethink tipping. The movement away from tipping has been slow. Some restaurants have tried it and succeeded. Others have tried and gone back to tipping.

In Ontario, server wages will go up by more than $3 per hour. Servers in most restaurants are making more money from tips than they are from the hourly wage. We've argued that past increases in minimum wage have actually hurt low-wage kitchen workers because the restaurant has to pay servers more too.

Our research from several years ago found that 75 per cent of respondents made more than $10 an hour in incremental wages from tips, 50 per cent earned more than $15 per hour and 25 per cent earned more than $20 per hour.

Eliminating tipping and paying a fixed wage (higher than minimum wage for servers) would provide the restaurants with a way to pay all staff a living wage without charging customers more. It wouldn't be easy, but the increase in minimum wage might provide additional impetus. I expect some restaurants will try it.

There has been some discussion of Ontario restaurants implementing a so-called "Wynne tax," a reference to provincial premier Kathleen Wynne. The tax would be 20 per cent of the bill to highlight to customers that the minimum wage increases are costing restaurants more.

It's unlikely it would work. It's difficult to highlight specific costs separately on a bill. Restaurants that tried it would likely see it decrease tips too.

No Servers?

Those that can will likely automate some functions. Restaurant Brands International, parent company of Tim Hortons and Burger King, is looking at self-serve ordering kiosks already. Tablet ordering at the table will certainly get more consideration. It's unlikely restaurants can take servers out of full-service restaurants entirely, but tablet ordering may allow operations to reduce the number of people they have on staff.

Some restaurants will close. Some have already announced closures based on minimum wage increases. People will lose their jobs. But this could actually increase the demand in restaurants that carry on.

Some have argued that we have too much capacity (too many seats) in the restaurant industry. Fewer total seats may mean more people in the remaining seats.

A Harvard University study evaluated what sorts of restaurants went out of business when minimum wages went up. Researchers evaluated Yelp and TripAdvisor reviews. Restaurants with good reviews were much less likely to go out of business. This suggests well-operated, customer-focused restaurants will retain diners and stay in business, but those that don't do so well on those fronts are at greater risk.

In the end, restaurants will find a way to adapt. It's a tough business, and restaurant operators have been forced to adapt before. They'll do it again—but diners will likely notice their efforts due to higher prices, smaller portion sizes and reduced hours.

> "Low-wage workers have to work
> longer hours just to achieve
> the standard of living that was
> considered the bare minimum almost
> half a century ago."

To Lift Full-Time Workers Out of Poverty, the Hourly Minimum Wage Must Be Raised to $15

David Cooper

In the following excerpted viewpoint, David Cooper begins with some history and philosophy of the federal minimum wage to provide context to the argument, then he points out that the US Congress has allowed the federal minimum wage to erode even as productivity has steadily increased. These conditions have meant that American workers are working harder and longer hours just to achieve a standard of living that a generation ago was considered the bare minimum. It also means that many Americans who work full-time jobs still live in poverty. The author notes that a minimum wage should be set at a level at which workers can live a decent life. David Cooper is a senior economic analyst at the Economic Policy Institute.

"Raising the Minimum Wage to $15 by 2024 Would Lift Wages for 41 Million American Workers," by David Cooper, Employment Policies Institute, April 26, 2017. Reprinted by permission.

As you read, consider the following questions:

1. How has an unchanged minimum wage affected low-wage workers over the last few decades?
2. Why would it not be sufficient to simply restore the minimum wage to what it was a generation ago?
3. What would be the ripple effect of a graduated increase?

The federal minimum wage was established in 1938, as part of the Fair Labor Standards Act (FLSA), to help ensure that all work would be fairly rewarded and that regular employment would provide a decent quality of life. In theory, Congress makes periodic amendments to the FLSA to increase the federal minimum wage to ensure that even the lowest-paid workers benefited from broader improvements in wage and living standards.

Yet for decades, lawmakers have let the value of the minimum wage erode, allowing inflation to gradually reduce the buying power of a minimum wage income. When the minimum wage has been raised, the increases have been too small to undo the decline in value that has occurred since the 1960s. In 2016, the federal minimum wage of $7.25 was worth 10 percent less than when it was last raised in 2009, after adjusting for inflation, and 25 percent below its peak value in 1968.

This decline in purchasing power means low-wage workers have to work longer hours just to achieve the standard of living that was considered the bare minimum almost half a century ago. Over that time, the United States has achieved tremendous improvements in labor productivity that could have allowed workers at all pay levels to enjoy a significantly improved quality of life (Bivens et al. 2014). Instead, because of policymakers' failure to preserve this basic labor standard, a parent earning the minimum wage does not earn enough through full-time work to be above the federal poverty line.

Restoring the value of the minimum wage to at least the same level it had a generation ago should be uncontroversial. But such a raise would be insufficient. The technological progress and productivity improvements that the country has achieved over the last 50 years have not benefited all of America's workers. This means lawmakers must strive to enact minimum wage increases that are bolder than the typical legislated increases in recent decades.

In April 2017, Sens. Bernie Sanders (I-Vt.) and Patty Murray (D-Wash.), and Reps. Bobby Scott (D-Va.) and Keith Ellison (D-Minn.) announced that they would introduce the Raise the Wage Act of 2017, a bill that would raise the federal minimum wage in eight steps to $15 per hour by 2024. Beginning in 2025, the minimum wage would be "indexed" to median wages so that each year, the minimum wage would automatically be adjusted based on growth in the median wage. The bill would also gradually increase the subminimum wage for tipped workers (or "tipped minimum wage"), which has been fixed at $2.13 per hour since 1991, until it reaches parity with the regular minimum wage.[1]

This report begins by providing historical context for the current value of the federal minimum wage and the proposed increase to $15 by 2024. It then describes the population of workers likely to receive higher pay under an increase to $15 by 2024, with detailed demographic data that refute a number of common misconceptions about low-wage workers. The report concludes with a discussion of the provisions of the Raise the Wage Act that would index the minimum wage to median wages, and gradually eliminate the subminimum wage for tipped workers.

This report finds that:

- A $15 minimum wage in 2024 would undo the erosion of the value of the real minimum wage that began primarily in the 1980s. In fact by 2019, for the first time in over 50 years, the federal minimum wage would exceed its historical inflation-adjusted high point, set in 1968.
- Gradually raising the minimum wage to $15 by 2024 would directly lift the wages of 22.5 million workers. On average, these low-wage workers would receive a $3.10 increase in their hourly wage, in today's dollars. For a directly affected worker

who works all year, that translates into a $5,100 increase in annual wage income, a raise of 31.3 percent. Another 19.0 million workers would benefit from a spillover effect as employers raise wages of workers making more than $15 in order to attract and retain their workforces.

- All told, raising the minimum to $15 in 2024 would directly or indirectly lift wages for 41.5 million workers, 29.2 percent of the wage-earning workforce.
- Over the phase-in period of the increases, the rising wage floor would generate $144 billion in additional wages, which would ripple out to the families of these workers and their communities. Because lower-paid workers spend much of their extra earnings, this injection of wages would help stimulate the economy and spur greater business activity and job growth.
- The workers who would receive a pay increase are overwhelmingly adult workers, most of whom work full time in regular jobs, often to support a family.
  - The average age of affected workers is 36 years old. A larger share of workers age 55 and older would receive a raise (16.1 percent) than teens (9.8 percent). More than half of all affected workers are prime-age workers between the ages of 25 and 54.
  - Although men are a larger share of the overall US workforce, the majority of workers affected by raising the minimum wage (55.6 percent) are women.
  - The minimum wage increase would disproportionately raise wages for people of color— for example, blacks make up 12.2 percent of the workforce but 16.7 percent of affected workers. This disproportionate impact means large shares of black and Hispanic workers would be affected: 40.1 percent of black workers and 33.5 percent of Hispanic workers would directly or indirectly get a raise.

- · Of workers who would receive a raise, nearly two-thirds (63.0 percent) work full time, nearly half (46.6 percent) have some college experience, and more than a quarter (28.0 percent) have children.
- · Four out of every 10 single parents who work (40.8 percent) would receive higher pay, including 44.6 percent of working single mothers. In all, 4.5 million single parents would benefit, accounting for 10.8 percent of those who would be affected by raising the minimum wage

- The workers with families—defined as a worker with a spouse or a child in the home—who would benefit are, on average, the primary breadwinners for their family, earning an average of 63.8 percent of their family's total income.
- A federal minimum wage increase to $15 in 2024 would raise wages for the parents of 19 million children across the United States, nearly one-quarter (24.0 percent) of all US children.
- Indexing the minimum wage to median wages would ensure that low-wage workers share in broad improvements in US living standards and would prevent future growth in inequality between low- and middle-wage workers.

[…]

The Minimum Wage in Context

Since its inception in 1938, the federal minimum wage has been adjusted through legislated increases nine times—from a nominal (non-inflation-adjusted) value of 25 cents per hour in 1938 to the current $7.25, where it has remained since 2009. These increases have been fairly irregular, varying in size and with differing lengths of time between increases. Yet aside from a few very brief deflationary periods in the post-WWII era, prices have consistently risen year after year. Each year that the minimum wage remains unchanged, its purchasing power slowly erodes until policymakers enact an increase. This haphazard maintenance of the wage floor has meant that low-wage workers of different generations or in different decades have been protected by significantly different wage standards.

[...]

A higher minimum wage would direct a portion of overall labor productivity gains into higher living standards for low-wage workers. It is not known precisely how much productivity in low-wage work has grown since the 1960s relative to overall productivity. However, low-wage workers today tend to be older (and are therefore likelier to have greater work experience) and are significantly more educated than their counterparts in 1968 (Mishel 2014a). To the extent that workers with more experience and greater education typically earn more than their younger and less-educated counterparts, we would expect low-wage workers today to earn more, not less, than what they earned in the previous generation. In this context, a pay increase for America's lowest-paid workers of 29 percent over the 56-year span from 1968 to 2024 is indeed modest when compared with projected overall productivity growth of 119 percent over the same period.[4]

The minimum wage is also a mechanism for combating inequality. As increased productivity has translated into higher wages for high-wage workers, a rising minimum wage ensures that the lowest-paid jobs also benefit from these improvements. This is the essence of the "fairness" implied in the name of the Fair Labor Standards Act, the act that established the minimum wage.

[...]

When set at an adequate level, the minimum wage also ensures that work is a means to a decent quality of life. In fact, the explicit purpose of the FLSA is to correct "labor conditions detrimental to the maintenance of the minimum standard of living necessary for health, efficiency, and general well-being of workers."[5] The federal poverty line is often cited as a proxy for the level of income needed for the general well-being of families. Researchers and policymakers have long acknowledged that, in reality, the poverty line is woefully inadequate as a measure of what is truly needed for a family to afford the basic necessities.[6] Yet even against this low bar, the federal minimum wage has rarely produced enough income for regular full-time workers, particularly those with children, to meet their needs.

[…]

Demographic Characteristics of Affected Workers

Raising the federal minimum wage to $15 by 2024 would lift pay for nearly one-third of American workers. The vast majority of workers who typically benefit from minimum wage increases do not fit the common portrayal of low-wage workers as primarily teenagers from middle-class families who are working part time after school, or stay-at-home mothers whose "secondary earnings" are inconsequential to their family's financial health.[7] As the subsequent sections show, increasing the minimum wage to $15 by 2024 would raise wages for millions of prime-age, full-time workers, many of whom are the primary breadwinners for their families.

[…]

Some opponents of raising the minimum wage contend that as a policy for reducing economic hardship, the minimum wage is ineffective because many poor people do not work. This is false. As explained in Gould, Davis, and Kimball (2015), the majority of poor people age 18 to 64 who can work (i.e., they are not in school, retired, or disabled) do work, and over 40 percent work full time. Moreover, increasing the minimum wage is an effective tool for reducing poverty. In a comprehensive review of the literature on the minimum wage's poverty-reducing effects, Dube (2013) finds that nearly all studies of this relationship show that raising the minimum wage significantly reduces poverty rates. In a recently released analysis of minimum wage increases from 1984 through 2013, Dube (2017) finds that for every 10 percent increase in the minimum wage, over the long run, the poverty rate is expected to decline by 5.3 percent.

A variation of this criticism is that the minimum wage is "poorly targeted" because some of the workers who would benefit from a minimum wage increase come from middle-class families. The fact that the minimum wage provides protection to workers at all levels of family income is a feature, not a bug, of the law. As a labor standard, the minimum wage prevents exploitation of workers, regardless of their family income level. No worker, no matter how wealthy his or her family, should have to work for unacceptably low wages. Moreover, the fact that some low-wage workers do come from middle-class families underscores the point that the erosion in the minimum wage's value over the past 45 years has hurt both low- and middle-income families.

[...]

The Importance of Affected Workers' Pay to Their Family's Total Incomes

Low-wage workers are sometimes characterized as "secondary earners," suggesting that their work earnings are discretionary or inconsequential to their family's financial health. The data show that this is not at all the case. Roughly half of all workers who would be affected by raising the minimum wage to $15 by 2024 are either married or has children, or both, and the average worker with a family who would benefit from increasing the minimum wage to $15 by 2024 is, in fact, the primary breadwinner for her family. Workers who would get a raise that are either married or have children earn, on average, 63.8 percent of their family's total income. Of these workers with families, 29.6 percent are the sole providers of their family's income.[15]

[...]

Indexing to Median Wages

After reaching $15 in 2024, the Raise the Wage Act would index the minimum wage to median wages so that in subsequent years, as wages throughout the workforce rise, the minimum wage would automatically be lifted to maintain its value relative to the median wage. This is different from how most minimum wage indexing has been done in the past. There are currently 18 states that have enacted indexing of their state minimum wages to changes in prices, typically as measured by changes in the Consumer Price Index (CPI). Indexing to prices prevents any erosion in the minimum's real (inflation-adjusted) value, thereby ensuring that low-wage workers can still afford the same amount of goods and services year after year. This is certainly advantageous to having no indexing; however, indexing to prices effectively legislates that the lowest-paid workers never see any material improvement in their quality of life. The real value of the minimum wage remains frozen, regardless of increases in overall labor productivity or technological advances that improve the country's ability to improve living standards.

In contrast, linking the minimum wage to median wages ensures that low-wage workers do not lose ground relative to typical workers. As Zipperer (2015b) explains, indexing to the median wage "links the minimum wage to overall conditions in the labor market." To the extent that productivity improvements and technological progress result in higher wages for the typical US worker, so too will minimum wage workers see their hourly pay rise.

[...]

Conclusion

Since its inception in the Great Depression, a strong minimum wage has been recognized as a key labor market institution that, if effectively maintained, can provide the foundation for equitable and adequate pay for American workers. However, the failure to regularly and adequately raise the federal minimum wage over the past five decades is one of several policy failures that have denied a generation of American workers more significant improvement in their quality of life. In fact, the erosion of the minimum wage has left low-wage workers today earning significantly less than their counterparts 50 years ago.

Raising the federal minimum wage to $15 by 2024 would take its value to a level that finally ensures full-time work is a means to escape poverty, and would provide tens of millions of America's lowest-paid workers with a substantial, long-overdue improvement in their standard of living. Past increases in the minimum wage have been too timid to preserve low-wage workers' standard of living, let alone allow them to share in the broader benefits of rising productivity and a growing economy. In contrast, the Raise the Wage Act is a bold proposal that would achieve these goals.

Automating future increases by indexing to growth in the median wage would ensure workers at the bottom of the wage scale are never again left behind as productivity improvements lead to broader improvements in wages. In addition, gradually raising and eliminating the separate lower wage for tipped workers would eliminate the disparities in labor protections and living standards that currently exist between tipped and non-tipped workers. These actions would significantly improve the well-being of millions of American workers and their families, and help to reduce long-standing race- and gender-based wage inequities.

Endnotes

1. It would also phase out the youth minimum wage, which allows employers to pay workers under 20 a lower wage for the first 90 calendar days of work (US Department of Labor Wage and Hour Division 2008a), and the subminimum wage for workers with disabilities, which allows employers, after receiving a certificate from the Wage and Hour Division of the Department of Labor, to pay workers with disabilities a lower wage (US Department of Labor Wage and Hour Division 2008b).

4. Overall productivity is measured as total economy productivity net depreciation. From 1968 to 2016, net productivity grew by 93 percent. Based on projections for productivity growth in CBO (2017), growth from 1968 to 2024 is expected to be 119 percent.

5. Fair Labor Standards Act of 1938.

6. See Gould and Wething (2013), who describe the various shortcomings of the federal poverty line and discuss alternative tools for measuring well-being.

7. See Cooper and Essrow (2015).

15. Author's calculation based on Current Population Survey Outgoing Rotation Group data, 2016.

Periodical and Internet Sources Bibliography

The following articles have been selected to supplement the diverse views presented in this chapter.

Andrew Bloomenthal, "Can a Family Survive on the US Minimum Wage?" Investopedia, June 20, 2021. https://www.investopedia.com/articles/personal-finance/022615/can-family-survive-us-minimum-wage.asp

Paul Boyce, "Why the Minimum Wage Can't Solve the Poverty Problem," Foundation for Economic Education, July 5, 2019. https://fee.org/articles/why-the-minimum-wage-can-t-solve-the-poverty-problem/

Evan Comen, "Jobs Don't Always Keep You Out of Poverty," *USA Today*, October 4, 2019. https://www.usatoday.com/story/money/2019/10/04/largest-working-poor-poverty-rates-jobs/40235285/

Matthew Desmond, "Americans Want to Believe That Jobs Are the Solution to Poverty. They're Not," *New York Times*, September 11, 2018. https://www.nytimes.com/2018/09/11/magazine/americans-jobs-poverty-homeless.html

Rebecca Hasdell, et al., "Millions of America's Working Poor May Lose Out on Key Anti-Poverty Tax Credit Because of the Pandemic," The Conversation, August 3, 2020. https://theconversation.com/millions-of-americas-working-poor-may-lose-out-on-key-anti-poverty-tax-credit-because-of-the-pandemic-141846

Edward Lempinen, "A $15 Minimum Wage Would Cost Jobs, Right? Probably Not, Economists Say," *Berkeley News*, March 18, 2021. https://news.berkeley.edu/2021/03/18/a-15-minimum-wage-would-cost-jobs-right-probably-not-economists-say/

Eric Morath, "Biden Wants a $15 Minimum Wage. Here's What People Say It Would Do to the Economy," *Wall Street Journal*, updated February 3, 2021. https://www.wsj.com/articles/biden-wants-a-15-minimum-wage-heres-what-people-say-it-would-do-to-the-economy-11612348201

David John Moratta, "Raising the Minimum Wage Hurts the Most Disadvantaged," *Forbes*, March 24, 2021. https://www.forbes.com /sites/davidmarotta/2021/03/24/raising-the-minimum-wages -hurts-the-most-disadvantaged/?sh=53c908d642dc

Annie Nova, "The Pandemic Is Driving Millions of America's 'Working Poor' to the Edge," CNBC, September 19, 2020. https:// www.cnbc.com/2020/09/19/coronavirus-how-the-pandemic -impacts-americas-working-poor.html

Eli Rosenberg, "CBO Report Finds $15 Minimum Wage Would Cost Jobs but Lower Poverty Levels," February 8, 2021. https://www .washingtonpost.com/business/2021/02/08/minimum-wage -hike-15-an-hour-by-2025-would-result-14-million -unemployed-nonpartisan-congressional-budget-office-says/

Michael Sainato, "Target Raised Wages. Then It Cut Workers' Hours and Doubled Their Workload," *The Guardian*, February 27, 2020. https://www.theguardian.com/business/2020/feb/27/target-cuts -hours-leaves-workers-struggling

OPPOSING
VIEWPOINTS®
SERIES

CHAPTER 2

Is Raising the Minimum Wage Unfair to Workers?

Chapter Preface

The primary reason for raising the minimum wage is to ensure that employers pay a fair, living wage to all workers. Virtually everyone agrees that if someone works full-time, they should be able to afford the basics: a place to live, food to eat. In this chapter, however, the viewpoints address the possibility that a minimum wage might actually be *unfair* to workers, that it might do more harm than good to the people it's meant to help. This strange contradiction involves a lot of assumptions about how the economy works, as well as how employers might respond to an increased minimum wage. For example, if faced with a mandated wage increase, would businesses lay off workers? Cut back on the hours of the workers they do employ? Or would they simply raise the prices on the goods they manufacture or sell? If they make the later response, would that mean a loss in profits that would eventually lead to layoffs anyway?

Because there are so many unknowns, much of this discussion is speculation. However, there are also case studies and research on the issue. In many of the following viewpoints, the authors cite research to back their claims, either that an increased minimum wage would do more harm than good or that it would be a net positive for workers. The problem is that economics is a soft science. It can be fiendishly difficult to design measurable criteria for studying the effects of any economic change or intervention. This means the authors of the viewpoints in this chapter have a lot to discuss. We begin with a viewpoint citing a Congressional Budget Office finding that a $15 minimum wage would likely increase unemployment. We end with one citing a lengthy list of studies showing that it wouldn't. In between are several other takes on the issue.

> *"An increase to a $15 minimum wage would not only slow recovery but would likely hurt many of the very workers it is intended to help."*

A $15 Minimum Wage Would Price Some Workers Out of the Market

Isabel Soto

In the previous chapter, we saw that the Congressional Budget Office has found that increasing the minimum wage would indeed reduce poverty, but it would likely also increase unemployment. In the following viewpoint, Isabel Soto examines the potential effect of a $15 minimum wage on the economic recovery and the workers such a wage increase is intended to help. Isabel Soto is director of labor market policy at the American Action Forum.

As you read, consider the following questions:

1. How does the context in which the author writes affect her argument?
2. How would an increased minimum wage disproportionately harm Black and Hispanic workers?
3. What alternative to an increased federal minimum wage does the author suggest?

"Examining the Effects of Raising the Federal Minimum Wage to $15," by Isabel Soto, American Action Forum, January 27, 2021. Reprinted by permission.

The Biden Administration has proposed raising the federal minimum wage from \$7.25 to \$15 an hour as part of its COVID-19 economic relief plan. Some believe that Congress could raise the minimum wage with a simple majority vote in the Senate by utilizing the budget reconciliation process. An increase in the minimum wage—particularly one as substantial as what is being proposed—would benefit some workers but harm others by pricing them out of the labor market. The labor supply side data indicate that there are millions of unemployed workers who are low skilled and have lower educational attainment. These workers would likely remain disconnected from work as a result of a \$15 minimum wage. On the demand side, many businesses face plummeting net revenues and even closing; this is particularly true of the small businesses already damaged by the COVID-19 recession that disproportionately hire those workers. An increase to a \$15 minimum wage would not only slow recovery but would likely hurt many of the very workers it is intended to help.

Consequences of Increasing the Minimum Wage

The consequences of rapid, large increases to the federal minimum wage are well documented, with much of the research finding negative employment effects. The Congressional Budget Office, for example, projected that an increase to a \$15 minimum wage by 2025 could mean an average of 1.4 million jobs lost, a fall in business revenues leading to a \$9 billion drop in real income, and increases in the prices of goods and services across the economy. The American Action Forum (AAF) has also analyzed the effects of increases in minimum wage. Additional evidence of the adverse effects of minimum wage increases can be found in Seattle's efforts to raise its wages. A National Bureau of Economic Research report found that the city's increase to a \$13 minimum wage in 2016 (up from \$11) reduced hours worked in low-wage jobs by 9 percent. Seattle's \$2 increase is small compared to what other states and localities would need to do if faced with a two-fold increase in the federal minimum wage; in most states, this would mean placing a wage floor close to the current median wage. Because wages across the country vary significantly by locality, it would be far more prudent to address wage changes in a more local manner rather than a federal mandate that risks putting smaller, already vulnerable employers out of business and hurting the workers minimum wage increases are intended to help. The COVID-19 pandemic would amplify the negative effects that increases would have on low-wage workers and small businesses.

Labor Supply and Unemployment

The pandemic has affected nearly every part of the nation's economy, but some industries and workers have disproportionately felt the negative consequences. Knowing which industries and types of workers are most impacted by the current economic situation can give a clearer picture of where a substantial increase to minimum wage would do the most damage and potentially leave more individuals without work.

While the Biden Administration has vocalized its intent to support low-income individuals and families, particularly those from Black and Hispanic communities, a federally mandated minimum wage of $15 would disproportionately hurt these workers. The devastating effect that the pandemic has had on communities of color has been explored at length. Black and Latino workers, for example, make up nearly a quarter of the service industry labor force and are less likely to be represented in managerial positions. In the leisure and hospitality industry, Black and Hispanic workers make up 13 and 24 percent of workers, respectively.

As shown here, the employment situation for Black and Hispanic workers has improved since unemployment reached its highest levels, but these groups are still disproportionately represented among the unemployed. A large increase to the

Unemployment by Race and Ethnicity[1]

WORKER RACE/ ETHNICITY	MAKING AT OR BELOW MINIMUM WAGE (PERCENT DISTRIBUTION)	PEAK PANDEMIC UNEMPLOYMENT (%)	DEC 2020 UNEMPLOYMENT (%)	DEC 2019 UNEMPLOYMENT (%)
Black	17.9**	16.8	9.9	5.9
Hispanic	18.2	18.9	9.3	4.2
White (non-Hispanic)	72.6**	13.6	6.0	3.2

** Estimates for the above race groups–White, Black or African American do not sum to totals because data are not presented for all races. Persons whose ethnicity is identified as Hispanic or Latino may be of any race.

federal minimum wage could price out of the labor force those currently unemployed and potentially lead to additional layoffs or job cuts.

Another segment of workers particularly at risk are those with a lower educational attainment. Bureau of Labor Statistics (BLS) data show that workers who did not graduate from

Unemployment by Educational Attainment[2]

EDUCATIONAL ATTAINMENT	MAKING AT OR BELOW MINIMUM WAGE (PERCENT DISTRIBUTION)	PEAK PANDEMIC UNEMPLOYMENT (%)	DEC 2020 UNEMPLOYMENT (%)	DEC 2019 UNEMPLOYMENT (%)
Less than High School Diploma	18.2	21.2	9.8	5.5
High School Graduates	34.1	17.3	7.8	3.8
Some College	34.9	15	6.3	2.8
Bachelor's Degree or Higher	12.7	8.4	3.8	2.0

high school were particularly affected by the pandemic, with unemployment rising to 21 percent and still at nearly double 2019 levels. In contrast, the unemployment rate for workers with a bachelor's degree or higher is returning to 2019 levels. Unsurprisingly, workers with lower educational attainment are more likely to be working at or below the minimum wage. Given that the United States does not have widely available up-skilling or reskilling programs and higher education is often prohibitively expensive, workers with low educational attainment and low skills will likely feel the effects of increased minimum wage the most.

Demand for Workers and the State of Small Businesses

The COVID-19 pandemic has driven many businesses—particularly small businesses—to close permanently or to operate on thin margins even as the economy begins to recover. Many of these businesses already face a challenging environment, where they have had to absorb costs associated with additional safety precautions and state-mandated business closures while losing revenue from reduced business.

Adding the cost of a $15 minimum wage could force the most vulnerable businesses to forgo hiring, reduce worker hours, cut jobs, or simply close altogether.

When businesses first began feeling the effects of COVID-19, layoffs were concentrated in industries that typically necessitated in-person service. The leisure and hospitality industry, for example, saw 40 percent unemployment at its peak, and according to 2019 BLS data had the largest concentration of low-wage workers. Other industries that have been significantly affected by the pandemic include mining, construction, transportation, and food services. While improvement has occurred, unemployment in these sectors remains high.

Given that these industries typically have large concentrations of low-wage workers, many of whom are currently experiencing

Wages and Unemployment in Industries Strongly Affected by the COVID-19 Pandemic[3]

INDUSTRY	AVERAGE HOURLY WAGE (NON SUPERVISORY)	DEC 2020 UNEMPLOYMENT (%)	DEC 2019 UNEMPLOYMENT (%)
Leisure and Hospitality	$14.57	16.7	5.0
Accommodation and Food Services	$13.84	16.4	5.0
Transportation and Warehousing	$22.95	9.3	2.8
Mining	$27.96	13.1	3.8
Construction	$29.64	9.6	5.0

unemployment, an increase in the minimum wage to $15 would add additional hurdles to rapid reopening and rehiring, driving long-term unemployment for the least educated and skilled workers.

Small Business Closures

The pandemic has forced many small businesses to close temporarily due to a lack of business and mandated closures; it also led to many businesses closing permanently. April 2020 saw the largest percent change in the number of open small businesses, a 44 percent decline from January 2020.

Of particular note are the changes that occurred in the leisure and hospitality industry, which in April 2020 saw a nearly 50 percent reduction in open small businesses relative to January 2020. This industry employs a large majority of workers who would be directly affected by changes to minimum wage, many of whom are likely still experiencing unemployment.

Percent Change of Small Businesses Open by Industry (Since Jan 2020)[4]

INDUSTRY	PEAK PERCENTAGE CHANGE IN OPEN SMALL BUSINESSES (APRIL 2020)	PERCENT CHANGE IN OPEN SMALL BUSINESSES (DEC 2020)
Leisure and Hospitality	-49	-48
Education and Health Services	-43	-21
Retail and Transportation	-38	-20
Professional and Business Services	-28	-16
All	-44	-30

As noted, closures due to reduced business and mandates understandably resulted in lost revenue; while many larger businesses were able to absorb the loss, many small businesses have had to permanently close or turn to layoffs as a cost-saving measure. While the Paycheck Protection Program loans, created as part of the Coronavirus Aid, Relief, and Economic Security Act, provided temporary relief to many, businesses continue to struggle.

Though revenues improved between April and December, the state of the leisure and hospitality industry remains unstable especially as cases continue to rise.

Given that the average non-supervisory wage in the leisure and hospitality industry is less than the proposed $15 minimum wage, those businesses would need to manage the impact of additional costs further reducing net revenue. An increase in the minimum

Percent Change in Small Business Revenue by Industry
(Since Jan 2020)[5]

INDUSTRY	PEAK PERCENTAGE CHANGE IN REVENUE (APRIL 2020)	PERCENT CHANGE IN REVENUE (DEC 2020)
Leisure and Hospitality	-72	-64
Education and Health Services	-58	-22
Retail and Transportation	-50	-19
Professional and Business Services	-32	-11
All	-50	-31

wage would force many small businesses to increase prices, likely reducing demand for goods and services, or to reduce hiring, cut worker hours, or eliminate jobs.

Conclusion

A federal minimum wage increase would exacerbate the economic harm already faced by many businesses and their workers. While those minimum wage workers who are able to keep their jobs would certainly benefit from the increase, many others risk additional harm. Particularly threatened are the large number of unemployed individuals who previously worked as low-wage workers in industries that have been most negatively affected by the pandemic. The demand for those workers to return during this time remains unclear. Adding a federally mandated cost in the form of increased minimum wage would lead to longer unemployment, reduced work hours or hiring, and increased layoffs for low-wage workers as businesses balance reduced revenues and increased costs.

Notes

1. https://www.bls.gov/web/empsit/cpseea06.htm; https://fas.org/sgp/crs/misc/R46554 .pdf; https://www.bls.gov/opub/reports/minimum-wage/2019/home.htm#cps_ mw_whe_char.f.1
2. https://www.bls.gov/news.release/empsit.t04.htm; https://www.bls.gov/opub/reports /minimum-wage/2019/home.htm#cps_mw_whe_char.f.1
3. https://www.bls.gov/web/empsit/cpseea31.htm; https://www.bls.gov/iag/
4. Economic Tracker (tracktherecovery.org)
5. Ibid.

> *"Additional income produced by a
> growing economy was going not to
> workers, but to capital—investors
> and employers."*

Wage Floors and Stronger Unions Are Necessary to Address Stagnant Wages

Kate Bahn

In the following viewpoint, written before the COVID-19 pandemic, Kate Bahn argues that wages did not recover along with everything else after the 2008 recession. Stagnant wages have been blamed on a so-called "skills gap," but the author maintains that the blame lies elsewhere. In fact, wages are not growing sufficiently even in high-skilled fields. The problem is not a skills gap, but the effects of weakened unions and a low minimum wage. Kate Bahn is director of labor market policy and interim chief economist at Equitable Growth.

As you read, consider the following questions:

1. How does the author explain the odd fact that the economy grew but wages did not?
2. What is the so-called "skills gap" discussed in this viewpoint?
3. What is "upskilling," and why is it opportunistic?

"'Skills Gap' Arguments Overlook Collective Bargaining and Low Minimum Wages," by Kate Bahn, Washington Center for Equitable Growth, May 9, 2019. Reprinted by permission.

As the US economy slowly but steadily recovered from the Great Recession beginning in 2009, Gross Domestic Product grew, employment rose, and the unemployment rate declined. These were all consistent with an economic recovery, but one very important metric has not caught up. Wages, seemingly defying the laws of labor supply and demand, remained essentially flat. The economy was growing, demand for workers was rising faster than the supply, yet the nominal price of their labor was not increasing any faster than inflation. As a result, the additional income produced by a growing economy was going not to workers, but to capital— investors and employers. And while real wage growth has begun to pick up in recent months, it is still below target for a tight labor market.

In the post-World War II era, as productivity rose, wages for US workers went right up with it. Workers enjoyed the fruits of their hard work, made ever more efficient and productive by improving technology. But in the 1970s, as the Economic Policy Institute has demonstrated, wages and productivity became decoupled. As the EPI figures show, productivity has risen fairly steadily since then, yet wages have stagnated.

Over time, one theory—which was advanced about the flattening of wages and today is almost accepted wisdom—was that wages were rising at a healthy clip for skilled workers; it was only relatively low-skilled workers for whom wages were flat. There were higher-skilled jobs available, the theory went, but not enough workers with those skills. Hence, the supposed "skills gap" between supply and demand for skills.

But if the problem of growing wage inequality were primarily a problem of skills, then to make wages grow, policymakers would need to reduce the skills gap. The way to do that, so the argument still goes, is for workers to become better educated and better trained by getting higher degrees and by learning new trades. And this should be a priority for government—to fund such skills acquisition across the age and educational spectrum.

Yet interestingly, and not coincidentally, among those supporting this interpretation of wage stagnation most aggressively were businesses. It was as though employers had nothing to do with setting those flat wages. And it was as though businesses had no responsibility to train their workers in new skills so they could earn higher wages. For businesses, fixing the skills gap rested on the shoulders of workers themselves, perhaps with support from the government by making education more accessible.

There's no question that investment in human capital—in education and training, in particular—should be a high priority. Such investments pay dividends for individuals, for the economy, and for society. Moreover, this is a shared responsibility of government, individuals, and, yes, businesses. But education and training are only a necessary condition for wage growth, not a sufficient one. Moreover, whether the amount of such investment was related to the flattening of wages is an entirely different matter.

Indeed, as the recovery nears its decade-long mark and the jobs market continues to tighten, wages have finally begun to move upward modestly because of a tightening labor market. But there is a way to go for wages to reach a level reflecting long-run productivity increases and to overcome historical wage disparities between groups of workers.

The Skills Gap Isn't the Problem

The skills gap has always been an interesting idea, but there has never been empirical evidence to back up the underlying theoretical foundation. While it's true that workers with more education tend to earn more, disparities by race and gender within education levels are still rampant. In recent years, some outstanding research has taken a look behind the curtain of this popular story.

In 2016, Alicia Sasser Modestino of Northeastern University, Daniel Shoag of Harvard University, and Joshua Balance of the Federal Reserve Bank of Boston found that a significant element of the alleged skills gap was inflated job requirements. These

THE MINIMUM WAGE HAS ALWAYS BEEN CONTROVERSIAL

The minimum wage is always politically controversial. Little wonder a cottage industry has sprung up in recent years examining the economic consequences of the minimum wage. Does a minimum wage harm the low-skill workers it's supposed to benefit? Or, is the minimum wage a savvy policy for raising the rewards to work?

While the economic research has focused largely on documenting the employment effects of higher minimum wages, that is too limited a perspective, according to NBER Research Associate David Neumark and co-author William Wascher. In "Minimum Wages and Training Revisited" (NBER Working Paper No. 6651), they broaden the investigation into a detailed look at the impact of minimum wage laws on job training. Theory suggests that minimum wages will reduce employer-offered on-the-job training because the tutoring is financed out of worker wages. Neumark and Wascher's analysis relies on variations in minimum wage laws from 1981 to 1991. They find that "...minimum wages reduce training aimed at improving skills on the current job, especially formal training." The cuts in training associated with a higher minimum wage are most apparent among 20- to 24-year-olds.

Still, the lure of a higher minimum wage might encourage low-skill or less-educated workers to get more schooling in order to qualify for a job. Indeed, the authors note that some advocates believe a higher minimum wage is a route toward a high-wage economy. Yet "there is no evidence that minimum wages raise the amount of training obtained by workers to qualify for their current job, and, indeed, there is some evidence that minimum wages reduce this kind of training as well." Among the many implications of their research, the authors argue, is that the data undermine the case for using minimum wages to encourage a "high-wage" path for the economy.

"Minimum Wages Discourage Training," by Chris Farrell, National Bureau of Economic Research, December 1998.

researchers showed that when the labor market was slack during the Great Recession and the years following, employers engaged in "opportunistic upskilling" by adding job requirements that they had not deemed necessary before. Those requirements tended to fall by the wayside as the recovery proceeded and the job market became more robust.

In 2018, Heidi Shierholz and Elise Gould of the Economic Policy Institute showed that real wages were not rising significantly even in high-skill occupations with very low unemployment. If there were a skills shortage, they argued, then wages would be rising in the occupations where those shortages existed. They noted that computer and mathematical science occupations—the skills for which often figure in conversations about skill shortages—had a low unemployment rate of 2.3 percent in 2018 but real wage growth of less than 1 percent.

Plus, there is a spate of evidence that a worker's level of education, while certainly important to wage levels, is not conclusive. Race, in particular, is shown to be a significant factor in wage differentials. A 2014 Center for Economic and Policy Research report by Janelle Jones (now of the Hub Project) and John Schmitt (a former Equitable Growth research director and now of EPI) showed that white college graduates recovered far more rapidly from the Great Recession than did black college graduates. One reason is that black college graduates, on average, are younger than white graduates, but this does not explain the entire disparity between the groups.

Another piece of evidence that a skills gap was not the cause of stagnating wages is related to the significant increase in the number of care-work jobs, which face a pay penalty owing to the societal devaluation of care work—not because it is not actually valuable, as shown in research by Equitable Growth grantee Nancy Folbre of University of Massachusetts Amherst and Paula England of New York University. Rachel Dwyer of The Ohio State University showed that care work specifically illustrates the problem of increasing job polarization. As the US population has aged, there has been a sharp rise in care-work employment, and it has been predominately in low-skill, low-wage jobs. While there are high-wage positions as well, there are not the kind of middle-wage jobs to which low-wage workers would gain access by gaining new skills.

Diminished Union Power and Low Minimum Wages Are the Problem

What, then, explains the decades-long stubbornness of wages, including in the years the US economy was recovering from the recession?

As a partial explanation, a growing number of researchers are pointing to monopsony—the power of individual firms in an increasingly concentrated economy to set wages, rather than the broader labor market setting wages through competition for workers. Douglas A. Webber of Temple University, in his 2015 paper "Firm Market Power and the Earnings Distribution," found labor supply elasticity to be lower than it would be in a competitive market, thus showing that firms were able to exercise greater power over the wages of their workers. As I've written previously, he found that "dynamic monopsony across the economy may be one of the reasons we experience high income inequality in the United States, and why most workers have not been able to share in the economic growth of the wealthiest nation."

Another important contributing factor is the steep, decades-long decline in union membership. In their working paper, "Unions and Inequality Over the Twentieth Century: New Evidence from Survey Data," Suresh Naidu of Columbia University, Henry S. Farber and Ilyana Kuziemko of Princeton University, and Daniel Herbst, now of the University of Arizona, concluded that there is a sustained wage premium for union membership, and that this premium is most significant for lower-wage workers. They concluded that there is a significant relationship between the level of US union membership and the level of inequality in the US economy.

Each of these explanatory factors for wage stagnation—the rise of monopsony and the decline of unions—points to the role of power in wage determination. Likewise, the wage disparities experienced by nonwhite workers and women who have equivalent education to their white and male counterparts is also due to structural power imbalances resulting from historical legacies of racism and sexism. If the current small increase in wage growth is to be sustained, not only in the current recovery but also when the economy inevitably slows, structural changes will be needed. In the imperfectly competitive monopsony model, employers are able to set wages below the marginal revenue productivity of labor. This deadweight loss can be reduced or eliminated by increasing minimum wages and through effective collective bargaining by unions against monopsonistic employers.

There is no denying the importance of education and training to long-term outcomes for workers. But that does not mean the solution to stagnant or inadequate wage increases lies in addressing a skills gap. To address the wage problem, Congress and regulators need to ensure that workers retain the ability to organize into unions, and unions need to have the power to bargain collectively—and effectively—to negotiate fair wage levels. In addition, policymakers need to establish wage floors that spill over into higher pay for workers along the distribution. Policies like these will compensate for power imbalances that have maintained wage stagnation.

> *"Although minimum wage laws can set wages, they cannot guarantee jobs."*

Minimum Wage Laws Harm Low-Skilled Workers

Sheldon Richman

In the following viewpoint, Sheldon Richman opens with data from Seattle that was mentioned in earlier viewpoints. Seattle's increased minimum wage appears to have resulted in fewer hours for low-skilled workers (a phenomenon we also saw in chapter 1). The author disregards the economic nuances and suggested fixes for this problem mentioned in the previous viewpoint and makes the case that quite simply the laws of supply and demand ensure that the minimum wage puts low-skilled workers out of work. Sheldon Richman is a freelance editor and author.

As you read, consider the following questions:

1. What is the law of supply and demand?
2. Why does the author support studies that he suggests are flawed?
3. How would the author of the previous viewpoint respond to this argument?

The movement to raise the national minimum wage to $15 an hour has suffered a blow with a new National Bureau of Economic Research working paper evaluating the recent experience in Seattle, Wash. The paper by Ekaterina Jardim and four other University of Washington economists indicates that Seattle's three-step hike in its minimum wage—from $9.57 to $15—is harming low-skilled workers.

The authors found that at $13 an hour, hourly wages in low-paying jobs rose 3.1 percent last year, but hours worked dropped 9.4 percent—3.5 million hours per quarter—for an average loss of $125 in wages per worker per month. Economist Mark Perry points out that things should only get worse with the "additional $2 an hour increase in the city's minimum wage that just took effect on January 1 of this year from $13 to $15 an hour for large employers."

In other words, as most economists have long predicted, the chief victims of minimum-wage laws are the supposed beneficiaries.

Oddly, the *Washington Post*'s story on the Seattle study, "A 'Very Credible' New Study on Seattle's $15 Minimum Wage Has Bad News for Liberals," states,

> The paper's conclusions contradict years of research on the minimum wage.... Economists have long argued that increasing the minimum wage will force some employers to let workers go. In 1994, however, economists David Card and Alan Krueger published research on minimum wages in Pennsylvania and New Jersey that contradicted this theory, motivating dozens of studies into the issue over the coming years.

In fact, many decades of empirical economic research have found net harm to low-skilled workers, illustrating what economic theory leads us to expect. As economist Linda Gorman writes in *The Concise Encyclopedia of Economics*:

> Most economists believe that minimum wage laws cause unnecessary hardship for the very people they are supposed to help.
>
> The reason is simple: although minimum wage laws can set wages, they cannot guarantee jobs....

Several decades of studies using aggregate time-series data from a variety of countries have found that minimum wage laws reduce employment.

Regarding Card-Krueger, Gorman points out that when their study of fast-food restaurants was redone using payroll records rather than unreliable telephone surveys, David Neumark and William Wascher found a drop in the number of fast-food jobs in New Jersey, where the minimum wage had increased. "Card and Krueger retreated from their earlier position," Gorman adds, but they still claimed what they termed "a small positive effect."

Just as Card and Krueger's study was criticized for methodological flaws, so is the UW paper being criticized. *The Post* notes, however, "Economists might not readily dismiss the new study as an outlier, however. The paper … makes use of more detailed data than have been available in past research, drawing on state records of wages and hours for individual employees."

The UW research contradicts a positive evaluation released a week earlier at the University of California–Berkeley. Michael Saltsman of *Forbes* notes that the city funded the Berkeley study after it had commissioned the UW one. Why? "Unfortunately for the Mayor's office," Saltsman writes, the UW researchers' "conclusions … were not uniformly positive." The Berkeley researchers were known for favoring minimum-wage increases.

Ironically, empirical studies on both sides of the controversy are subject to methodological objections because any economic situation is complex: countless factors influence events, and isolating the cause of an effect makes finding a needle in a haystack child's play. Data don't speak for themselves: they must be interpreted with a theory. A rise in the minimum wage might be followed by increased employment of unskilled workers, but correlation is not causation. Other factors could offset the rise in the wage, which is why economists like to say "other things equal" when talking about change.

Does that mean we cannot know whether the minimum wage is beneficial or harmful? Not at all. We have economic theory to guide us—specifically the law of demand. As anyone who shops knows, as the price of a good or service rises, other things equal, the quantity demanded tends to fall. A rise in the minimum wage, assuming low-skilled workers have not suddenly become more productive, will tend to harm those workers: fewer workers may be hired; some may be replaced by machines or higher-skilled, higher-paid workers; hours may be cut; fringe benefits and amenities may be curtailed or eliminated. "In other circumstances," the UW study says, "employers may conclude that the work of least-paid workers need not be done at all."

There is simply no reason to think the law of demand does not apply to labor markets. Minimum-wage advocates often claim that increases are good for business. Why, then, must employers be forced?

To raise wages, the government need only stop obstructing competition, saving, and investment, which make workers more productive.

> *"Many economists have backed away
> from the argument that minimum
> wage [laws] lead to fewer jobs."*

Research Shows That Minimum Wage Increases Do Not Cause Job Loss

Holly Sklar

In the previous viewpoint, the author focused on the unintended consequence of decreased hours for workers when the minimum wage is raised. In the following viewpoint, Holly Sklar outlines research on real-life minimum wage increases that shows that contrary to many claims, increasing the minimum wage is not likely to cause job losses and business closures. Holly Sklar is a policy analyst and founder and CEO of Business for a Fair Minimum Wage

As you read, consider the following questions:

1. Why might the cost of increasing its minimum wage be modest to many companies?
2. How might decreasing labor turnover save businesses money?
3. Why do you think the author added the list of research to the end of her article?

E xtensive research refutes the claim that increasing the minimum wage causes increased unemployment and business closures. (See research list below.)

The buying power of the minimum wage reached its peak in 1968 at $12.71, adjusting for the cost of living in 2021 dollars. The unemployment rate went from 3.8% in 1967 to 3.6% in 1968 to 3.5% in 1969. The next time the unemployment rate came close to those levels was after the minimum wage raises of 1996 and 1997. *Business Week* observed in 2001, "Many economists have backed away from the argument that minimum wage [laws] lead to fewer jobs."

Numerous states raised their minimum wages above the federal level during the 1997-2007 period when the federal minimum wage remained stuck at $5.15. Research by the Fiscal Policy Institute and others showed that states that raised their minimum wages above the federal level experienced better employment and small business trends than states that did not.

A series of rigorous studies by the Institute for Research on Labor and Employment (IRLE) beginning in 2008 significantly advanced the research on minimum wage employment effects. *Minimum Wage Effects Across State Borders* compared all neighboring counties in the US located on different sides of a state border with different minimum wage levels between 1990 and 2006 and found no adverse employment effects from higher minimum wages.

The IRLE report, *Spatial Heterogeneity and Minimum Wages: Employment Estimates for Teens Using Cross-State Commuting Zones,* found "no discernable disemployment effect, even when minimum wage increases lead to relatively large wage changes." *Do Minimum Wages Really Reduce Teen Employment?* analyzed the 1990-2009 period. Carefully controlling for more factors than previous minimum wage studies, the researchers found the answer is no.

In a 2013 report, *Why Does the Minimum Wage Have No Discernible Effect on Employment?*, the Center for Economic and Policy Research analyzed extensive research conducted since

THE FEDERAL MINIMUM WAGE HURTS LOW-SKILLED WORKERS

We find that increases in the minimum wage significantly reduced the employment of low-skilled workers. By the second year following the $7.25 minimum wage's implementation, we estimate that targeted individuals' employment rates had fallen by 6.6 percentage points (9%) more in bound states than in unbound states. The implied elasticity of our target group's employment with respect to the minimum wage is -1, which is large within the context of the existing literature.

We next estimate the effects of binding minimum wage increases on low-skilled workers' incomes. The 2008 SIPP [Survey of Income and Program Participation] panel provides a unique opportunity to investigate such effects, as its individual-level panel extends for 3 years following the July 2009 increase in the federal minimum wage. We find that this period's binding minimum wage increases reduced low-skilled individuals' average monthly incomes. Relative to low-skilled workers in unbound states, targeted individuals' average monthly incomes fell by $90 over the first year and by an additional $50 over the following 2 years. While surprising at first glance, we show that these estimates can be straightforwardly explained through our estimated effects on employment, the likelihood of working without pay, and subsequent lost wage growth associated with lost experience. We estimate, for example, that targeted workers experienced a 5 percentage point decline in their medium-run probability of reaching earnings greater than $1500 per month.

"The Federal Minimum Wage Increase Hurt Many Low-Skilled Workers," by David Henderson, The Library of Economics and Liberty.

the 1990s. They conclude that "the minimum wage has little or no discernible effect on the employment prospects of low-wage workers." They note that "the cost shock of the minimum wage is small relative to most firms' overall costs." They explore various means of adjustment by employers such as increased worker productivity and diminished wage gap between lower and higher paid employees and say, "probably the most important channel of adjustment is through reductions in labor turnover, which yield significant cost savings to employers."

Minimum wage research was strengthened significantly by Cengiz, Dube, Lindner and Zipperer in *The Effect of Minimum Wages on Low-Wage Jobs*, published in *The Quarterly Journal of Economics* in 2019. They "estimate the effect of minimum wages on low-wage jobs using 138 prominent state-level minimum wage changes between 1979 and 2016 in the United States" and "find that the overall number of low-wage jobs remained essentially unchanged over the five years following the increase."

In evaluating minimum wage increases, it's important to remember that workers are also customers. Increasing the minimum wage increases consumer spending. As we say in *Raising the Minimum Wage to $15 Helps Small Business*, "Raising the minimum wage is a very efficient way to boost business and the economy because it puts money in the pockets of people who most need to spend it." Raising the minimum wage pays off for businesses in other ways. Businesses that pay low wages typically have high employee turnover. With increased wages, businesses see lower employee turnover, which reduces hiring and training costs; decreased employee financial stress and increased morale; increased productivity; lower error and accident rates; less product waste; and better customer service.

Selected Research in Chronological Order

Lawrence F. Katz and Alan B. Krueger, The Effect of the Minimum Wage on the Fast Food Industry, National Bureau of Economic Research, February 1992.

David Card, Using Regional Variation in Wages to Measure the Effects of the Federal Minimum Wage, *Industrial and Labor Relations Review*, October 1992.

David Card and Alan Krueger, *Myth and Measurement: The New Economics of the Minimum Wage* (Princeton, NJ: Princeton University Press, 1995).

Jared Bernstein and John Schmitt, Economic Policy Institute, Making Work Pay: The Impact of the 1996-97 Minimum Wage Increase, 1998.

Jerold Waltman, Allan McBride, Nicole Camhout, Minimum Wage Increases and the Business Failure Rate, *Journal of Economic Issues*, March 1998.

A Report by the National Economic Council, The Minimum Wage: Increasing the Reward for Work, March 2000.

David Card and Alan B. Krueger, Minimum Wages and Employment: A Case Study of the Fast-Food Industry in New Jersey and Pennsylvania: Reply, *American Economic*

Review, December 2000 (in this reply, Card and Krueger update earlier findings and refute critics).

Holly Sklar, Laryssa Mykyta and Susan Wefald, *Raise the Floor: Wages and Policies That Work for All of Us* (Boston: South End Press, 2001), Ch. 4 and pp. 102-08.

Fiscal Policy Institute, States with Minimum Wages above the Federal Level Have Had Faster Small Business and Retail Job Growth, March 2006 (update of 2004 report).

John Burton and Amy Hanauer, Center for American Progress and Policy Matters Ohio, *Good for Business: Small Business Growth and State Minimum Wages*, May 2006.

Liana Fox, Economic Policy Institute, Minimum Wage Trends: Understanding past and contemporary research, November 8, 2006.

Paul Wolfson, Economic Policy Institute, State Minimum Wages: A Policy That Works, November 27, 2006.

Arindrajit Dube, Suresh Naidu, Michael Reich, The Economic Effects of a Citywide Minimum Wage, *Industrial & Labor Relations Review*, July 2007.

Jerold L. Waltman, *Minimum Wage Policy in Great Britain and the United States* (New York: Algora, 2008), pp. 17-19, 132-136, 151-162, 178-180.

Sylvia Allegretto, Arindrajit Dube, Michael Reich, Do Minimum Wages Really Reduce Teen Employment?, Institute for Research on Labor and Employment, Univ. of CA, Berkeley, June 2008.

Arindrajit Dube, T. William Lester, Michael Reich, Minimum Wage Effects Across State Borders: Estimates Using Contiguous Counties, Institute for Research on Labor and Employment, August 2008. Published by *The Review of Economics and Statistics*, November 2010.

Michael F. Thompson, Indiana Business Research Center, Minimum Wage Impacts on Employment: A Look at Indiana, Illinois and Surrounding Midwestern States, *Indiana Business Review*, Fall 2008.

Sylvia Allegretto, Arindrajit Dube, Michael Reich, Spatial Heterogeneity and Minimum Wages: Employment Estimates for Teens Using Cross-State Commuting Zones, Institute for Research on Labor and Employment, June 25, 2009.

Sylvia Allegretto, Arindrajit Dube, Michael Reich, Do Minimum Wages Really Reduce Teen Employment? Accounting for Heterogeneity and Selectivity in State Panel Data, Institute for Research on Labor and Employment, June 21, 2010. Published by Industrial Relations, April 2011.

John Schmidt, Why Does the Minimum Wage Have No Discernible Effect on Employment?, Center for Economic and Policy Research, February 2013.

Michael Reich, Ken Jacobs and Miranda Dietz (eds.), *When Mandates Work: Raising Labor Standards at the Local Level* (Berkeley: University of California Press) 2014.

Michael Reich, The Troubling Fine Print in the Claim That Raising the Minimum Wage Will Cost Jobs (Response to CBO report), *Think Progress*, February 19, 2014.

Michael Reich, No, a Minimum-Wage Boost Won't Kill Jobs (Response to CBO report), *Politico*, February 21, 2014.

Michael Reich, Ken Jacobs, Annette Bernhardt, Local Minimum Wage Laws: Impacts on Workers, Families and Businesses, Institute for Research on Labor and Employment, March 2014.

Dale Belman and Paul J. Wolfson, The New Minimum Wage Research, W.E. Upjohn Institute for Employment Research, *Employment Research*, April 2014.

Dale Belman and Paul J. Wolfson, *What Does the Minimum Wage Do?*, W.E. Upjohn Institute for Employment Research (book), 2014.

Center for Economic and Policy Research, 2014 Job Creation Faster in States That Raised the Minimum Wage, June 2014

Center for Economic and Policy Research, Update on the Thirteen States That Raised Their Minimum Wage, August 2014.

Daniel Kuehn, The Importance of Study Design in the Minimum Wage Debate, Economic Policy Institute, September 2014.

Justin Wolfers and Jan Zilinsky, Higher Wages for Low-Income Workers Lead to Higher Productivity, Peterson Institute for International Economics, January 13, 2015.

Peterson Institute for International Economics, Raising Lower-Level Wages: When and Why It Makes Economic Sense, April 2015.

Alan Stonecipher and Ben Wilcox, Minimum Wage Policy and the Resulting Effect on Employment, Integrity Florida, July 20, 2015.

Paul J. Wolfson and Dale Belman, 15 Years of Research on US Employment and the Minimum Wage, Tuck School of Business, December 2015.

National Employment Law Project, Raise Wages, Kill Jobs? Seven Decades of Historical Data Find No Correlation Between Minimum Wage Increases and Employment Levels, May 2016.

Executive Office of the President, Raising the Minimum Wage: A Progress Update, October 2016.

Jared Bernstein, "New evidence of the minimum wage doing what it's supposed to do: Help low-wage workers," Washington Post, March 8, 2018.

Small Business Administration, Small Business Facts: Why Do Business Close?, May 2018.

Sylvia Allegretto, Anna Godøy, Carl Nadler, Michael Reich, The New Wave of Local Minimum Wage Policies: Evidence from Six Cities, Institute for Research on Labor and Employment, September 6, 2018.

Doruk Cengiz, Arindrajit Dube, Attila Lindner, Ben Zipperer, The Effect of Minimum Wages on Low-Wage Jobs, The Quarterly Journal of Economics, August 2019.

Jason Bram, Fatih Karahan, Brendan Moore, Minimum Wage Impacts along the New York-Pennsylvania Border, Liberty Street Economics, Federal Reserve Bank of New York, September 25, 2019.

Greg David, "NY Fed: Minimum wage hikes didn't kill jobs," Crain's New York Business, September 25, 2019.

Arindrajit Dube and Attila S. Lindner, City Limits: What do Local-Area Minimum Wages Do?, National Bureau of Economic Research, October 2020.

Anna Godøy and Michael Reich, Are Minimum Wage Effects Greater in Low-Wage Areas?, Institute for Research on Labor and Employment, September 2020. Published by Industrial Relations in 2021.

Doruk Cengiz, Arindrajit Dube, Attila S. Lindner, David Zentler-Munro, Seeing Beyond the Trees: Using Machine Learning to Estimate the Impact of Minimum Wages on Labor Market Outcomes, National Bureau of Economic Research, January 2021.

Holly Sklar and Alissa Barron-Menza, Raising the Minimum Wage to $15 Helps Small Business, Business for a Fair Minimum Wage, February 24, 2021.

> "[An inadequate income] increases susceptibility to psychological stress, malaise, illness and disease."

Raising the Minimum Wage Is a Health Issue

Utibe Effiong

In the following viewpoint, Utibe Effiong argues that low wages directly affect public health. Research has shown that people with low household income are less likely to have health insurance, to put a priority on preventative care, and to seek out proper nutrition and other things that lead to a healthy lifestyle. The author notes that during the COVID-19 pandemic, people receiving unemployment benefits actually made more money than those with minimum-wage jobs. Raising the minimum wage can increase the health of the nation. Utibe Effiong is a board certified internal medicine physician and public health scientist at MidMichigan Health, University of Michigan.

As you read, consider the following questions:

1. What is the difference in life expectancy between the richest and poorest 1% of US men?
2. How is employment linked to self-esteem?
3. Why do unemployment benefits pay more than a minimum wage job?

Congress just missed one of its best shots at improving health when the Senate failed to advance a bill that would have raised the minimum wage to US$15 an hour. Study after study has linked higher income to better health.

Consider that a well-paying job, by definition, increases household income. That, in turn, means increased access to good nutrition, heat and a safe environment. It also means adequate health care. With that job, you'll likely make more visits to primary care doctors, dentists and specialists who work in preventive care.

An inadequate income does none of these things. Instead, it increases susceptibility to psychological stress, malaise, illness and disease. This is one reason those who move off welfare benefits and gain employment improve their well-being.

I am not an economist. But I am a physician and public health scientist. I can tell you that research shows that a well-paying job translates to a longer life. For example, researchers in 2016 found that the richest 1% of men in the US lived 14.6 years longer on average than the poorest 1% of men.

Employment Benefits

Numerous studies show employment is linked to self-esteem, purpose and identity. It provides relationships, social connections, social status and regular productive activity; a job is an integral part of a person's identity. Its loss threatens that identity, which is why unemployment typically causes a decline in mental health. When compared with their employed counterparts, unemployed Americans are far more likely to receive a diagnosis of depression.

One study found that people with a disability who were employed were less likely to have frequent mental distress, including anxiety and depression, than those with a disability who were not employed (18% vs. 40%). This finding held up even when accounting for demographics and individual characteristics.

A Possible Solution

Many economists have long criticized unemployment benefits because of their negative impact on the willingness to work. The average unemployment benefit is $320 weekly; the amount varies by state. The American Rescue Plan, recently passed to provide economic aid to million of Americans hit hard by the pandemic, adds an additional $300 to unemployment benefits through Sept. 6.

Compare that to the current federal minimum wage: $7.25 an hour. That's $290 for a 40-hour week, less than what unemployment benefits pay. That means, for millions of Americans, being employed means less income. With the federal supplement, 63% of workers currently make more on unemployment than they would with a minimum-wage job. Reduce the federal supplement to only $100 a week, and 25% of the workforce would still make more on unemployment.

Which raises the question: Why not increase the minimum wage—at least enough to make it more than unemployment benefits? That way, more people would be motivated to seek jobs.

That may not happen soon, if at all. President Biden's plan to raise the federal minimum wage to $15 per hour was not a part of the $1.9 trillion COVID-19 aid package. And it's true there's a downside: Raising the minimum wage can reduce the number of jobs available. A Congressional Budget Office estimate on Biden's proposal says the raise would lift 900,000 people out of poverty, but it would also kill 1.4 million jobs over four years.

That said, people who are fit to work should be encouraged to seek, not shun, employment. With unemployment benefits more than the basic minimum wage in many states, we are sending the wrong message to millions. There's more to a higher minimum wage than just more money. It also means more happiness, better health and a longer life.

Periodical and Internet Sources Bibliography

The following articles have been selected to supplement the diverse views presented in this chapter.

Ben Bergman, "Unions Have Pushed the $15 Minimum Wage, But Few Members Will Benefit," NPR, February 10, 2015. https://www.npr.org/2015/02/10/384980527/unions-have-pushed-the-15-minimum-wage-but-few-members-will-benefit

Greg Daugherty, "How the Minimum Wage Impacts Unemployment," Investopedia, updated March 26, 2021. https://www.investopedia.com/articles/personal-finance/013015/how-minimum-wage-impacts-unemployment.asp

Drew DeSilver, "The US Differs from Most Other Countries in How It Sets Its Minimum Wage," Pew Research Center, May 20, 2021. https://www.pewresearch.org/fact-tank/2021/05/20/the-u-s-differs-from-most-other-countries-in-how-it-sets-its-minimum-wage/

Arindrajit Dube, "No, a $15 Minimum Wage Won't Cost 1.4 Million Jobs," *Washington Post*, February 24, 2021. https://www.washingtonpost.com/outlook/2021/02/24/minimum-wage-economic-research-job-loss/

Gillian Friedman, "Once a Fringe Idea, the $15 Minimum Wage Is Making Big Gains," *New York Times*, December 31, 2020. https://www.nytimes.com/2020/12/31/business/economy/minimum-wage-15-dollar-hour.html

Brett Goldberg, "A $15 Minimum Wage Sounds Good but Has Unintended Consequences," *Entrepreneur*, July 30, 2018. https://www.entrepreneur.com/article/317508

Rachel Greszler, "Biden's COVID Stimulus Plan to Double Minimum Wage Will Hurt the People He Wants to Help," NBC News, February 3, 2021. https://www.nbcnews.com/think/opinion/biden-s-covid-stimulus-plan-double-minimum-wage-will-hurt-ncna1256547

Ken Jacobs, "The Public Cost of a Low Federal Minimum Wage," The Berkeley Labor Center, January 14, 2021. https://laborcenter.berkeley.edu/the-public-cost-of-a-low-federal-minimum-wage/

Annie Lowrey, "The Counterintuitive Workings of the Minimum Wage," *The Atlantic*, January 29, 2021. https://www.theatlantic .com/ideas/archive/2021/01/counterintuitive-workings -minimum-wage/617861/

Lily Roberts and Ben Olinsky, "Raising the Minimum Wage Would Boost an Economic Recovery—and Reduce Taxpayer Subsidization of Low-Wage Work," Center for American Progress, January 27, 2021. https://www.americanprogress.org /issues/economy/news/2021/01/27/495163/raising-minimum -wage-boost-economic-recovery-reduce-taxpayer-subsidization -low-wage-work/

Emma Stokic, "Raising the Minimum Wage Would Both Help and Hurt," News Decoder, April 21, 2021. https://news-decoder.com /raising-the-u-s-minimum-wage-would-both-help-and-hurt/

Bruce Western and Jake Rosenfeld, "Unions, Norms, and the Rise in US Wage Inequality," *American Sociological Review*, August 4, 2011. https://www.asanet.org/sites/default/files/savvy/images /journals/docs/pdf/asr/WesternandRosenfeld.pdf

OPPOSING
VIEWPOINTS®
SERIES

CHAPTER 3

Would Raising the Minimum Wage Harm Businesses?

Chapter Preface

The viewpoint authors in the previous chapter debated whether raising the minimum wage would hurt workers, the very people it's designed to help. The viewpoints in the following chapter ponder whether an increased minimum wage will harm businesses.

When businesses are harmed in some way—particularly financially—employees often bear the brunt. Therefore, some of the same issues discussed in chapter 2 arise in this chapter. Here, however, the focus is on how businesses might or might not suffer from an increased minimum wage. Some experts offer suggestions for how business owners might offset any potential harm.

One wrinkle in the issue of raising wages came along in 2020: the COVID-19 pandemic. The pandemic raised the stakes for both workers and businesses, particularly restaurants and other businesses that serve in-person clientele. When people were no longer able to gather, many of these businesses suffered. Some went under. And of course, many of their workers lost their jobs. This highlighted both the urgency of paying people enough so that they are not living on the raw edge of survival and also on the importance of supporting businesses so that they will have jobs to offer and can weather emergencies such as a pandemic.

Some believe that increasing the minimum wage would be too much of a burden on small businesses and would force many to close their doors. Others believe that an increased minimum wage might actually be a boon to small businesses.

As we saw in the previous chapter, the data can be fuzzy and the outcomes can't totally be predicted. But viewpoint authors on all sides of the issue take a hard look and marshal evidence to support their views.

| "Multiple studies also show that a higher minimum wage would benefit employers by boosting morale and productivity and decreasing employee turnover and absenteeism.

A $15 Minimum Wage Is Risky for Small Businesses

Roy Maurer

In the following viewpoint, Roy Maurer begins by outlining the difficulties small businesses might face with a $15 minimum wage. He then presents ideas for how those businesses might actually benefit and closes with the suggestion that minimum wages might be best determined at the local level. Roy Maurer covers talent acquisition, immigration, HR technology, and labor markets for the Society for Human Resource Management.

As you read, consider the following questions:

1. How has the pandemic complicated the discussion of raising the minimum wage?
2. What percentage of US employers are small businesses employers?
3. Why might it be better to base minimum wages on local economies rather than nationally?

"Will a $15 Minimum Wage Hurt Small Businesses?" by Roy Maurer, SHRM, March 16, 2021. Reprinted by permission.

S mall businesses have been especially hard hit during the COVID-19 pandemic. That's why some believe this is an inopportune time to pursue raising the federal minimum wage to $15 an hour by 2025, as Democrats in Congress have proposed. But advocates of the Raise the Wage Act say that lower-income workers have also been struggling during the pandemic and the federal minimum wage is long overdue for an increase.

The introduction of the legislation resets the stage for debating the challenges and benefits of raising the minimum wage and the impact the policy would have on small employers.

The federal minimum wage was last raised—to $7.25—in 2009. Just over 1 million workers earned wages that were at or below the minimum wage in 2020, according to the Bureau of Labor Statistics.

A Trade-Off

The dilemma facing federal lawmakers was expressed by Rep. Dean Phillips, D-Minn., during a recent hearing on the issue called by the House Committee on Small Business.

"According to the Congressional Budget Office, the [Raise the Wage Act] will likely raise wages for 27 million Americans, raise almost a million people out of poverty and increase aggregate wages for low-wage workers by over $300 billion over the next decade," he said. "Unfortunately, the same study also projects that this policy could cost 1.4 million jobs … and the loss of some small businesses."

Phillips said he hears concerns from constituents like the owner of the Original Pancake House in Plymouth, Minn. "Like so many businesses which rely on public gathering to succeed, his is barely hanging on. His restaurant—like all restaurants—runs on thin margins during the best of times, and he is deeply concerned that a $15 minimum wage will mean he will have to cut jobs if he hopes to stay open."

Rep. Elizabeth Ann Van Duyne, R-Texas, said she couldn't think of anything more devastating to small businesses as they try to recover from the economic effects of the pandemic. "Small-business owners have told me that increasing the minimum wage will have a disastrous impact on them," she said. "Many said they would have to close their doors immediately, and others said they would have to choose between shutting down or replacing their workers with automation."

Phillips said he believes there are ways to "mitigate the negative impacts of such a policy while maximizing the positive impacts of raising wages for millions of Americans."

Job Losses, Business Closures

Opponents of increasing the minimum wage to $15 argue that it will burden small businesses—which make up 99 percent of all employers—with increased labor costs and result in layoffs, expediting automation or going out of business.

"Employers cannot have their labor costs increase by up to 100 percent without significant disruptions to their operations," said Rachel Greszler, a research fellow at the Heritage Foundation in Washington, D.C. "Responses to a $15 federal minimum wage will vary depending on their industries and unique circumstances, but their options include eliminating positions, cutting employee hours, reducing benefits, automating or outsourcing jobs, or closing down."

Greszler added that even employers of middle-wage workers may be subject to wage pressure. "In order to attract and retain the workers they need, employers have to maintain a hierarchy of wages based on experience and productivity. They cannot pay shift managers the same rate as entry-level workers."

Ian MacLean, the owner of Highland Landscaping in Southlake, Texas, and chair of the US Chamber of Commerce Small Business Council, said his company's lowest-wage earners currently make $11 per hour. "If the lowest-wage earners are increased to $15 per hour, every one of my employees currently making $15 per hour or more would, justifiably, want their hourly rates increased commensurate with their skills, experience and tenure above the new $15 per hour employees."

Greszler noted that some employers will respond to an increase in the minimum wage by replacing low-income workers with machines.

MacLean agreed that to mitigate the effects of a minimum-wage hike to $15, "we would fast-track automation solutions and eliminate most of our entry-level and lesser-skilled labor positions."

"These small businesses are the same as households," Greszler said. "If we were faced with paying twice the rent or twice the mortgage, we would have to make adjustments. Small-business owners tell me that they're taking out lines of credit during this pandemic because they care so much about their workers and they don't want to lay them off."

Higher Retention, Productivity

Proponents of the wage increase say that it will return low-wage workers to a standard of living considered the bare minimum decades ago, turning back the erosion of the value of the minimum wage after inflation.

Those making the federal minimum wage now make 30 percent less in inflation-adjusted pay than federal minimum-wage workers did 53 years ago, said Heidi Shierholz, senior economist and director of policy at the Economic Policy Institute in Washington, D.C.

"Had the minimum wage kept pace with labor productivity growth since 1968, the minimum wage would have been $21.69 in 2020, and … would be $23.53 in 2025," she said. "Affected workers who work year-round would earn an extra $3,300 a year—enough to make a tremendous difference in the life of a supermarket clerk, home health aide or fast-food worker who today struggles to get by on less than $25,000 a year."

The Raise the Wage Act also indexes the minimum wage to median wages. "By establishing regular, predictable increases to the minimum wage that are linked to overall wage growth, the proposed legislation improves the ability of the minimum wage to reduce inequality," Shierholz said. "A rise to $15 an hour would reverse decades of growing pay inequality between the lowest-paid workers and the middle class, and indexing future increases would prevent any future growth in that gap."

She added that multiple studies also show that a higher minimum wage would benefit employers by boosting morale and productivity and decreasing employee turnover and absenteeism.

That's what Punch Neapolitan Pizza co-owner John Puckett is counting on. The St. Paul, Minn.-based pizza chain currently pays an average of $13 per hour for starting wages and plans to move to $15 per hour by 2022, as directed by city mandate.

"We're trying to figure it out," Puckett said of the impact of the rising minimum wage on his business. "One of our key business strategies has been to recruit and hire the best employees, and central to that strategy has been paying more than our competitors and well above legal minimums to ensure we attract and retain the best people," he said. "Employee retention is about two and half times longer than industry average," he added.

Paying workers higher minimum wages is a priority for the company but comes at a cost, he said. "Our store-level labor cost is significantly higher than industry average. But since our business strategy is not to maximize short-term profit, but to build a company that will last generations, we think the extra money we spend on labor is money well-spent."

Locality-Based Pay

Some on both sides of the aisle agree that a single, nationwide federal minimum wage may not be the best solution. "Different regions with different economic conditions should not have the same wage policy," said Ryan Young, a senior fellow at the Competitive Enterprise Institute in Washington, D.C.

That's because of the widely varying cost of living across different parts of the country. "In high-cost Manhattan, for example, these trade-offs may barely be visible at a $15 minimum wage, because wages there are already in that range," Young said. "In smaller towns where costs and wages are lower, the trade-offs would be severe."

In Mississippi, for example, $15 per hour is the median wage. "Imposing a $15 minimum wage on Mississippi would be like imposing a $35.74 minimum wage on Washington, D.C., the equivalent of more than $74,000 per year," Greszler said.

She added that the best solution would be to use a locality-based wage system tied to the median wage, taking care not to disproportionally impact lower-cost areas negatively. "States and cities are free to set their own policies, and most already have," Young said. "Twenty-nine states currently have minimum wages well above the current federal minimum, and many cities have their own citywide minimum wages beyond state requirements that don't impose on communities with lower living costs."

"They will pivot. They will innovate. They will find a way to get their products and services out the door less expensively and more profitably."

Innovation and Technology Will Save Small Businesses

Gene Marks

In the following viewpoint, Gene Marks argues that raising the minimum wage to $15 is exactly what small businesses need. The author starts by giving an example of something that happened because of the COVID-19 pandemic and worked out much better than employers had expected: working from home. An increased minimum wage would likewise be a pleasant surprise for businesses, he writes. Innovation and new technology will keep small businesses afloat—and even prospering—after the wage increase. Gene Marks is founder of the Marks Group, a small-business consulting firm.

As you read, consider the following questions:

1. How does increased technology benefit business owners and management, according to the viewpoint?
2. What are some of the ways the author predicts small businesses will adapt to an increased minimum wage?
3. Why does the author seem thrilled about firing workers?

"Why a $15 Minimum Wage Is Exactly What Small Businesses Need," by Gene Marks, The Hill, February 10, 2021. Reprinted by permission.

Back before the pandemic, many small business owners I know were inundated with requests from their employees to work from home. And many of them resisted.

Well, the pandemic changed that. Business owners, forced by government shutdowns and fear of the virus, sent their employees home to work. And guess what? They did. "I admit I was wrong," one client recently told me. "If there's anything positive that's come out of this ordeal, it is that I've realized that working from home is a viable option for my employees, and a good benefit to provide." This development wasn't ground-breaking. The technology already existed. The pandemic merely accelerated a trend that was already taking place.

Something similar will happen if Congress raises the federal minimum wage to $15 per hour. I say, please do it and do it as fast as possible. Why? Because a higher minimum wage is the medicine that small businesses need. Like working from home, this legislation will force us all to do what we should have been doing in the first place: Get rid of our unskilled hourly employees and replace them with technology.

Because that is what will happen. A higher minimum wage will cause a significant bump in our overall compensation costs. It won't just be entry level. When you raise the minimum, all wages will eventually need to be increased correspondingly to keep levels on par.

So how do you think small business owners will respond? Will they run their businesses at a lower income level? Will they shut down? Perhaps, some will. But most will respond as entrepreneurs have responded for thousands of years. They will pivot. They will innovate. They will find a way to get their products and services out the door less expensively and more profitably. And they will do this with technology. Technology that already exists and will come down in price as the demand for it skyrockets.

Grocery stores will reduce their staff and automate like Amazon Go, allowing shoppers to pick a product off the shelf, scan with their phone and leave, with inventory levels monitored by sensors and automatically re-ordered.

Retail stores will add more self-service kiosks and bring in robots with cute names like "Marty" (Giant Food Stores) and "Pepper" (Softbank Solutions) to answer questions, give directions, clean up messes and check on products. They will also install automatic biometric scanners and facial recognition devices like these to provide security and reduce shoplifting. Customers will be enticed to make more use of their mobile apps to get questions answered and get recommendations instead of asking a bored sales clerk making $15 an hour. Sellers of cars and real estate will send augmented reality headsets like Microsoft's HoloLens 2 to prospective customers where they can get the full experience and make buying decisions without a salesperson.

Restaurants will install robotic chefs like Miso Robotic's Flippy that can flip burgers and operate a deep fryer; or use Autec Inc.'s Maki Maker ASM865A, which "produces rice sheets of various thickness and sizes for sushi rolls, sushi burrito, sushi pizza, sushi taco and more"; or a fully functioning "robotic restaurant" like the one opening in Illinois that will essentially embody 10 restaurants by providing pizza, burgers, chicken wings, Italian, Portuguese, Mediterranean, Indian, Chinese, Thai and Mexican food, all cooked up using "Chef Nala," an AI-driven robot. They will use cleaning robots, which will probably do a better job than their employees. They will certainly continue to leverage self-ordering and self-paying apps to minimize wait staff involvement and, therefore, minimize wait staff.

Manufacturers will terminate their line workers and replace them with robotic arms like the ones made by Universal Robots. Warehouse managers like those at logistics company DSV will use drones to check on inventories while others will deploy driverless, autonomous forklifts like the ones made by Mitsubishi Logisnext to find, retrieve and deliver items.

More small businesses will leverage artificial intelligence solutions already available by many software companies to automatically and without human involvement answer customer questions, follow up on sales calls, send sample products and check on the status of orders in process. Publishers will lay off staff in lieu of automatic story-generators.

The firms that make all of these technologies are very careful to say that these things won't "replace" workers. They'll just "enhance productivity" or "work alongside" existing staff. That's baloney. This stuff will absolutely replace workers. And what a delight this will be for many of us.

Why? Because we won't have to pay as much for health insurance or put away as much money for someone else's retirement. We will no longer be frustrated as frequently when someone doesn't show up to work as promised. We will happily deal with less drug problems and fights on our premises. Work scheduling, union organization, safety issues and payroll forms will be much less of a concern. We will be able to spend more time serving our customers and less time worrying about discrimination, harassment or other misbehaviors.

With a $15 an hour minimum wage, tomorrow's small businesses will have fewer employees, more technology, higher profits, fewer headaches and less stress. Like working from home, we've resisted doing this so far because many of us are too lazy or risk-averse. We've managed to eke out our profits and continue to do things the old way despite these rising costs. We've been reluctant to invest in new technologies. But that won't be the case going forward. We will do what we have to do in order to continue to make money and provide for our families.

> "Workers that earn higher wages
> are less likely to arrive late or miss
> work. They also tend to be more
> invested in their job, working harder
> and committing fewer employee
> conduct infractions."

Small Businesses Benefit When Wages Rise

Zoe Willingham

In the following viewpoint, Zoe Willingham agrees that a wage increase will benefit workers. The author argues that an increased minimum wage would result in an increase in spending, a clear benefit for businesses, because workers would be able to purchase household necessities they couldn't afford before the increase. In addition, she says that when workers are paid a fair wage, they are more productive and better employees. Zoe Willingham is a research associate for economic policy at the Center for American Progress.

As you read, consider the following questions:

1. What would minimum wage workers be likely to do with their increased wages?
2. How does increased pay increase production?
3. How will reducing turnover benefit employers?

For nearly a year now, small business owners have been struggling to keep their heads above water. As Congress looks for solutions to help the country recover from the COVID-19 crisis, supporting small businesses must be a priority and one of the best ways to do this is by raising the minimum wage to $15 an hour.

About a third of business owners report that the pandemic has had a large negative effect on their operations, with small business revenue down more than 30% compared with before the coronavirus made it to the United States. Overall, there are 34% fewer small businesses currently operating in the United States than at this time last year. Small businesses are the backbone of the US economy, employing nearly half of all workers.

Increased Spending

A $15 minimum wage will drive increased consumer spending to the benefit of small businesses. At the same time, workers making a fair wage are able and willing to work harder and be more productive, generating more value for business operators. These factors are just a few of the reasons that studies show that raising the minimum wage grows the whole economy with negligible job loss.

Even before the pandemic brought the country to its knees, the substandard minimum wage in the US presented a major structural economic weakness. Since it was last raised to $7.25 in 2009, inflation has eroded the spending power of the minimum wage by 17%—so a minimum wage worker today is earning just 83 cents for every dollar they earned 12 years ago.

For context, today, a full-time, minimum-wage workers cannot afford to rent a two-bedroom apartment anywhere in America. Even in Boise, Idaho—one of the most affordable cities in the United States—a two-worker household must make at least $15.94 per hour to support a child.

Raising the minimum wage would provide instant relief to struggling Americans and correct longstanding inequities. A minimum-wage increase would take a bite out of the gender pay

STUDY SHOWS $15 MINIMUM WAGE HURTS SMALL BUSINESS

A study from the National Bureau of Economic Research found that higher minimum wages adversely impacted small businesses, the *Wall Street Journal* reports. "As the federal minimum wage rose from 1989-2013, small businesses in affected states suffered 'lower bank credit, higher loan defaults, lower employment, a lower entry and a higher exit rate,'" the *Journal*'s editorial board wrote.

A trio of professors from the Georgia Institute of Technology analyzed data from states with a higher minimum wage than the federal standard against a variety of benchmarks. For example, for every $1 bump in the minimum wage above the federal level, loan amounts through the Small Business Administration fell 9% in those states. "Business entries fell 4% in the year the minimum wage went up. A year later, business exits rose 5%," the *Journal* wrote.

The study also found that restaurants and retail businesses suffered more because of their reliance on low-skilled workers. The study authors concluded "that increases in the federal minimum wage worsen the financial health of small businesses in the affected states."

"Study Shows $15 Minimum Wage Hurts Small Business," convenience.org, December 18, 2019.

gap, as women still earn 18% less than men. People of color—especially women of color—are more likely to work low-wage jobs.

32 Million Would Benefit

An estimated 32 million Americans would see their incomes rise, if the minimum wage were increased to $15 an hour—providing an instant boost to the economy by stimulating consumer spending. A $15 minimum wage by 2025 would generate $107 billion in higher wages for workers. A $1 an hour raise to a minimum wage worker increases annual household spending by $2,080.

Minimum-wage workers, more than anyone, are likely to spend their raise on household necessities that they were previously unable to afford like repairs and electronics. Research also shows that much of the increased spending would go to the small businesses that are hurting most—restaurants.

In addition to spurring increased demand, higher wages return dividends to employers in the form of a more productive workforce—offsetting much of the predicted payroll costs. Workers that deal with stresses related to poverty are unable to perform their best work and they are more likely to fall ill and call in sick. In contrast, workers that earn higher wages are less likely to arrive late or miss work. They also tend to be more invested in their job, working harder and committing fewer employee conduct infractions.

Paying higher wages also reduces the significant costs associated with employee turnover, such as recruitment, administrative work, and training. These costs total about one-fifth of the worker's annual salary, which, for an employee paid the federal minimum wage, exceeds $3,000.

Unfounded Fears of Job Losses

Critics of raising the minimum wage often try to stoke fears by arguing that a minimum wage hike will result in higher unemployment. But an exhaustive body of economic research disproves this. Studies of places that have increased the minimum wage have found insignificant impacts on the number of jobs, positive or negative.

Even sharp increases in the minimum wage have a minimal impact on employment levels. In the absence of major job losses, a $15 minimum wage would result in increased earnings among low-wage workers and a reduction in poverty and inequality as a result.

Lawmakers must recognize a $15 minimum wage as a crucial part of any post-pandemic economic recovery plan. Sens. Bernie Sanders, Patty Murray, and Chuck Schumer, along with their House colleagues Reps. Bobby Scott and Pramila Jayapal, introduced a provision into the American Rescue Plan—which is supported by

69% of business owners—that would raise the minimum wage to $15 gradually, starting at $9.50 in June and reaching $15 in 2025.

It would also eliminate the subminimum wage for tipped workers, who make $2.13 an hour, and disabled workers, who make $3.34 an hour. If the proposed minimum wage increase is enacted, it would give a raise to a total of 32 million workers and set the country on a path to equitable economic growth. It is especially urgent to act to raise the wage now to recognize the essential services that many low-wage workers provide during this time of crisis.

Raising the minimum wage to provide instant relief to workers and supplying urgent grants and other financing to small businesses like the American Rescue Plan proposes will help the economy work better for everyone.

At a time when so many businesses are struggling, we can't afford to suppress wages and with it, consumer spending. A $15 an hour minimum wage is essential to supporting small businesses and building a strong, long-lasting economic recovery.

> "[Increasing a minimum wage] is
> a complicated issue with many
> potentially serious implications for
> the future of our state as well as our
> lowest-skilled workers."

A Minimum Wage Increase Will Hurt Small Business and the Working Poor

Mark Alesse and Matthew Guilbault

In the following viewpoint, Mark Alesse and Matthew Guilbault offer a historic look at the minimum wage debate, from many years ago when the state of New York was debating a minimum wage increase. As you will see, the debate has not changed much over the years. The authors made then what is still a familiar argument: that a minimum wage increase would hurt small businesses and workers. They do offer a few unique twists, though. They say that an increased wage is unnecessary in part because the state of New York has plenty of programs for the poor. Mark Alesse is an op-ed writer and former business lobbyist. Matthew Guilbault is an attorney and associate director of state government affairs for the pharmaceutical company Novartis.

As you read, consider the following questions:

1. What do the authors mean when they say an increase in the minumum wage would put upward pressure on the entire wage structure?
2. What, according to the viewpoint, is organized labor's position on the increase?
3. Do the authors believe a minimum wage increase would cause a drastic shift?

The issue of increasing New York State's minimum wage is again receiving considerable attention in the state capitol in Albany. And at first blush, a lot of New Yorkers stopped on the street would probably agree with the general idea of putting more money into the pockets of the working poor. Even small-business owners may well think that putting more money into the hands of their poorer customers is a good idea. But raising the minimum wage is not the same as delivering more income into the hands of people with low-skill jobs.

In fact, it is a complicated issue with many potentially serious implications for the future of our state as well as our lowest-skilled workers. So, when something like a hike in the minimum wage is proposed—something that sounds simple, intuitive and benevolent—responsible citizens should still take a step back and ask: Who really pays for the increase? The answers may surprise you.

In 1999, New York hiked the state minimum wage to $5.15 per hour and permanently tied it to the federal rate. This placed New York State on par with every other state that links its minimum wage to the federal wage and eliminated the problems caused when competing states have differing wage laws. It leveled the playing field and placed the issue of a minimum wage where it belongs—with the federal government.

Nevertheless, organized labor is now pushing hard for a $1.60—or 31 percent—increase in the state's minimum wage, notwithstanding the competitive disadvantages for business that would come from leapfrogging the federal rate.

A higher minimum wage puts strong upward pressure on the entire wage structure, which is the real reason that unions support it. But as any first-year economics major will tell you, if you tax something (in this case, jobs) or increase its cost, you end up with less demand for that thing. Can a state with one of the most expensive business climates in the nation, that has 300,000 unemployed and has lost 100 manufacturing jobs a day for the past five years, afford a new round of generalized wage inflation? The unions ought to think this through more thoroughly.

Perhaps most surprising, though, is big labor's indifference to the question of whether or not a hike in the minimum wage would really help the working poor and whether we can afford its wider social and economic impacts. Research from Michigan State University, for example, found that increases in the minimum wage encourage more teenagers to leave school and enter the workplace, displacing lower-skilled workers from their jobs.

Raising the minimum wage will work to deprive the working poor of job opportunities. Those most affected will be single parents, developmentally disabled persons, school dropouts and recent immigrants with poor language and reading skills. If you price entry-level labor higher than its real value, jobs will not be available for people whose skills are limited.

Then there is the impact on small businesses, considered by many to be the engine of growth and opportunity in the American economy. A small increase of $1.60 per hour would cost a bake shop with ten clerks and bakers over $30,000 per year, not counting the increases that a higher payroll brings in the costs of workers compensation insurance, unemployment insurance, Social Security taxes, Medicare taxes and even liability insurance in some cases. This is money that most small employers simply do not have. So, what will they do? Lay off workers, increase prices, or both.

When you consider that businesses with fewer than 100 employees create the majority of new jobs in New York, and that small business has created about two-thirds of the net new jobs in the United States since 1970, the proposal to hike the minimum begins to look less attractive.

Small businesses in New York are struggling against a tide of steadily rising costs. To reverse this trend and stimulate growth and jobs we must work to reduce the costs of doing business. Increasing the minimum wage at a time when we can least afford it just adds to the problem.

Now, is the sky going to fall if New York increased its minimum wage? Would we see dramatic layoffs and skyrocketing unemployment overnight? Probably not. But given that state spending, debt and taxes are already too high, the increase would hurt.

The final reason for opposing an increase is that it is not necessary. New York offers a wide array of generous programs, like the Earned Income Tax Credit, that provide cash assistance to encourage people to work without the negative impacts of a hike in the minimum wage. Other assistance comes from the Child and Dependent Care Credit, the federal Child Tax Credit, the Home Energy Assistance Program, and the Real Property Tax Circuit Breaker. Health benefits are provided through programs like Child Health Plus, Family Health Plus, Healthy NY and Medicaid. Nutritional assistance comes from Food Stamps, the Special Supplemental Nutrition Program for Women, Infants, and Children (popularly known as WIC) program, and school breakfast and lunch programs. A college tuition tax credit also aids low-income families.

In 2003, the state and federal earned income tax credit was worth $5,465 per year for New York families making no more than twice the poverty level, providing over $700 million to the state's working families and individuals. With the tax credit counted, the effective hourly wage for a single parent with two children is $7.77 per hour (well above the wage rate sought by the Working

Families Party). Add in the value of food stamps, free school meals and health insurance and the effective value of a minimum wage job tops $14 per hour.

New York today generously helps its most needy residents— and in ways that do not damage small businesses or destroy job opportunities for teens and low-skilled people. Goodwill toward those who are less fortunate than us is natural—but it should not cause us to turn off our minds and end up spreading far more ill than good.

"A sizable body of economic research
makes clear, raising wages on the
bottom of the economy boosts
consumption, and thus supports
the growth of local economies—
something that's desperately needed
to help our communities recover from
the COVID-19 recession."

A $15 Minimum Wage Could
Help Restaurants and Other
Hard-Hit Small Businesses

Xavier de Souza Briggs and Russell Jackson

In the following viewpoint, Xavier de Souza Briggs and Russell Jackson bring us back into the modern debate. After debunking some myths about the proposed wage increase, the authors of this viewpoint go on to explain why a $15 minimum wage might actually strengthen businesses and help the economy recover from damage done by the COVID-19 pandemic. Xavier de Souza Briggs is a social scientist and policy expert affiliated with the Brookings Institution. Russell Jackson is a chef and restaurant owner.

"How a $15 Minimum Wage Could Help Restaurants and Other Hard-Hit Small Businesses," February 22, 2021. This post was originally published on brookings.edu by Xavier de Souza Briggs and Russell Jackson.

As you read, consider the following questions:

1. How was Republican senator Joni Ernst trying to trap Senate Democrats, according to the authors?
2. What are some of the myths about a $15 minimum wage discussed in this viewpoint?
3. Why are conservatives beginning to support a phased-in minimum wage increase?

A funny thing happened on the Senate floor in the wee hours of February 5. As senators worked through a series of amendments in the "vote-a-rama" to advance President Joe Biden's $1.9 trillion rescue package, Sen. Joni Ernst (R-Iowa) moved to strike any provision raising the federal minimum wage to $15 per hour this year. And none other than progressive lion Sen. Bernie Sanders (I-Vt.) rose to agree.

Pundits theorized that Ernst sought to trap Democrats, especially those from battleground states, into voting in favor of a minimum wage increase while the nation is still in the throes of the pandemic. But that's not congressional Democrats' position: Sanders and his allies support raising the minimum wage gradually, over a four-year period. In the end, no Democrats opposed Ernst's amendment.

The belief that Democrats want to dramatically and immediately raise the federal minimum wage—a belief the National Restaurant Association has eagerly fueled—isn't the only myth floating around about the proposal. Critics also declare that increase is only popular with progressives and that it will be a "job killer" for restaurants and other hard-hit small businesses, especially in lower-wage regions.

One of us runs a restaurant in a very high-cost market, so we understand concerns that raising the minimum wage might limit hiring or even drive more restaurants and other small companies out of business. But we need to get some facts straight.

First of all, raising the minimum wage isn't just a progressive position. There is now robust bipartisan support among voters for a significant increase in the federal minimum wage, which has not budged in a dozen years. In November, Florida voters approved an increase to the state minimum wage by a margin 11 points wider than Donald Trump's victory there. (Florida became the first state in the South, and eighth in the nation, to approve a gradual hike to $15.) Meanwhile, a Quinnipiac poll conducted in late January found that 61% of Americans favor the increase to $15 at the federal level.

A new Brookings analysis shows that pre-COVID-19, about half of workers earning less than $15 an hour were essential workers—a share that is likely higher now because of the pandemic's disproportionate effects on low-wage occupations. Voters across the spectrum have come to agree that it is simply not possible for workers—essential or otherwise—to survive on the federal minimum of $7.25 an hour or the state wage floors close to that.

But it's even less possible to survive on restaurant and other service work that relies on tips and is still paid a subminimum rate: $5 an hour or less in 38 states. Heavy reliance on tips rather than wages meant that for many workers laid off during the pandemic, total earnings were too low to even qualify them for unemployment insurance, as labor researchers at the University of California at Berkeley found last year.

Over 110,000 restaurants have shuttered during the pandemic, and Black restaurateurs and other owners of color—along with their workers—have been hit especially hard. But just as voters have realized that the minimum wage in America is a poverty sentence, leaders in the restaurant business—the nation's largest source of private sector jobs—are waking up to the fact that the industry will not survive unless it changes dramatically. On this point in particular, the restaurant industry is a microcosm of the American economy.

Many restaurants must raise wages to attract and retain workers, who face new safety risks as well as the loss of income from a big drop in tips. Evidence shows that raising wages can cut

Problems with Minimum Wage Increases

Minimum wage increases can have severe effects for small businesses. Increases in payroll expense often require small business owners to raise consumer prices on goods and services or reduce business costs. Payroll is often the highest expense for most small businesses. An increase in minimum wage may result in small businesses laying off employees. Employee layoffs are usually the first option as consumers may react negatively to an increase in product prices.

Minimum wage increases can also create negative situations for employees. Wage increases can push the employee's annual income into a higher tax bracket, of imposing a higher marginal tax rate on the individual. Minimum wage employees usually have lower wealth than other individuals in the economic marketplace. Tax liability increases can quickly erode the wealth of an individual living on minimum wage. Employees will also face higher payroll taxes, such as Social Security or Medicare, which can also reduce their immediate income.

Governments increasing minimum wage levels often create a distortion in free market economies. Free market economies are usually driven by the economic theory of supply and demand. Businesses

expensive employee turnover in half and trigger a shift to new business models, as Seattle and other local markets show. This adaptation—which is a crucial part of the future of retail more generally—is just one thing that pessimistic economic projections of the effects of a federal minimum wage hike (like that by the Congressional Budget Office) ignore or downplay.

What's more, tipping and the cruel logic of a subminimum wage are vestiges of slavery. After emancipation, employers in the South mobilized to keep Black labor as cheap as possible, winning the legal right to have workers in key occupations (such as waitressing) survive on customer tips rather than employer-paid wages. To this day, food servers' reliance on tips makes restaurant have a demand for employees and attempt to fill this demand from the available supply of individuals in the economic marketplace. Each party agrees to specific wages for a certain level of service. Minimum wage laws can create higher wages than companies are willing to pay for specific employee services.

Small businesses may also face increasing wages across the board. Minimum wage increases often bring unskilled or lower-level employee wages closer to the pay for individuals with technical or expert abilities. Business owners may need to consider raising these individual's wages to compensate for minimum wage increases. Higher-paid employees may also feel slighted by the government's ability to increase the minimum wage and leave other wage levels to free market standards.

Significant minimum wage increases can drive companies into dangerous financial situations. Retail stores, fast food restaurants, hotels and similar industries often rely on minimum wage individuals for completing several business tasks. Governments that continually increase minimum wage require businesses in these industries to pay more money for the same amount of employee service. If companies are unable to increase prices or reduce expenses, they may face liquidation or bankruptcy as a result from the wage increase.

"Problems with Minimum Wage Increases," by Osmond Vitez, *Houston Chronicle*.

customers very powerful, contributing to the worst incidence of reported sexual harassment of any industry.

A phased-in move to one fair wage, with tips supplementing rather than replacing a robust base wage of at least $15 per hour nationwide, is now critical. And it's not just industry icons like Danny Meyer and José Andrés who have come out in favor of such a move, but also Main Street employers and a national network of hundreds of restaurateurs organizing for fair wages as part of industry innovation. Last year, even McDonald's announced that it would not oppose the raise.

Minds are also changing across the capital markets that have done so much to drive short-term thinking about what's good for business. A new policy package created by a commission of conservative and progressive leaders from business, investment, economic research, and other fields has endorsed the move to $15 and one fair wage as the law of the land, emphasizing that capitalism needs to work for everyone. "The time for virtue-signaling is over," wrote the commission, which one of us serves on.

Finally, this is not just about fairness to workers. As a sizable body of economic research makes clear, raising wages on the bottom of the economy boosts consumption, and thus supports the growth of local economies—something that's desperately needed to help our communities recover from the COVID-19 recession. Let's recall that Franklin Roosevelt and Congress created the federal minimum wage during the Great Depression.

It's time for the Senate to back a phased-in raise to the minimum wage and end the subminimum tipped wage, which is both racist and sexist. The evidence shows that we can offer dignity to millions of low-income workers and boost the economy at the same time.

> *"Small businesses can reap several benefits from a higher minimum wage that may offset the increased payroll costs."*

Small Businesses Get a Boost from a $15 Minimum Wage

Zoe Willingham

In the following viewpoint, Zoe Willingham explains how the COVID-19 pandemic affected working families. The author argues that helping working families would also help businesses, which are also suffering because of the pandemic. In addition, the entire economy could benefit, as low-wage workers are more likely to spend their increases than high-wage earners, resulting in a boost to local economies. Zoe Willingham is a research associate for economic policy at the Center for American Progress.

As you read, consider the following questions:

1. According to the viewpoint, how will the impact of an increased minimum wage offset increased payroll costs?
2. How will an increased minimum wage help boost the economic recovery?
3. What effect will an increase in the minimum wage have on demand?

The coronavirus pandemic pulled the rug out from under working families seemingly overnight. In total, nine months into the pandemic, the number of unemployed workers reached more than 10.7 million, leaving countless families hungry.[1] In October 2020, more than 1 in 10 households with school-age children were experiencing food insecurity.[2] Though the initial relief provided by the weekly federal supplement of state unemployment insurance, expanded access to unemployment insurance, and the $1,200 direct payments kept some families afloat temporarily—with 18 million people boosted out of poverty in April—a total of 8 million people sunk below the poverty level from May to September 2020.[3]

But even before the mass unemployment resulting from the deadly public health crisis, the economy faced a major structural problem: The federal minimum wage was last raised in 2009. Since then, the rising cost of living has eroded the value of the minimum wage by more than 17 percent.[4] The disparity between the minimum wage and the current cost of living is so large that there is not a single US state in which a minimum wage worker can afford to rent a two-bedroom home.[5] This chasm is even starker for tipped workers, who make $2.13 per hour, and workers with disabilities, who earn just $3.34 per hour.[6] The result is an economy that does not work. Before the pandemic hit, 140 million people already lived near or below the poverty line.[7]

For the United States to achieve a meaningful economic recovery that lifts up all families, Congress must raise the federal minimum wage to $15 per hour, including for tipped workers and workers with disabilities. Raising the minimum wage would benefit small businesses and the economy at large. While critics of a fair wage argue that a $15 minimum wage would put a heavy burden on small businesses, economic literature demonstrates that these concerns are not borne out by the facts.

Small businesses across the country are in dire need of assistance to weather the remainder of the pandemic and rebound during the recovery. The number of small businesses currently operating is down almost 34 percent compared with January 2020.[8] Almost one-third of small businesses surveyed by the US Census Bureau in early January 2021 reported that the pandemic has had a "large negative effect" on their operations.[9] Small businesses are a crucial part of the US economy, employing about one-third of the workforce, according to the most recent available data.[10] As a result, small businesses are a crucial part of the recovery and need meaningful federal aid to rebuild.

The Paycheck Protection Program (PPP), which extended loans to businesses to keep their employees on the payroll, was quickly exhausted by the onslaught of entrepreneurs and business owners seeking assistance, leaving some out in the cold—particularly Black business owners.[11] The stress that small business owners face is real, prompting some business groups to lobby for delaying the implementation of several state and local minimum wage increases.[12] However, it's direct financial support to small businesses and entrepreneurs—not shortchanging workers—that is going to help them weather this storm.

Policymakers need not choose between a $15 minimum wage and small-business recovery. Research shows that these ends are not at odds. Minimum wage increases during recessions are not uncommon. Indeed, the minimum wage was first adopted during the Great Depression, when mass unemployment suppressed wages far below subsistence levels and the necessity of a federal wage floor became painfully evident. In fact, a $15 minimum wage, combined with further federal relief for small businesses, will benefit small and medium-sized enterprises in the long run. Economic literature has found that increases in worker productivity, reductions in turnover, and aggregate increases in consumer spending offset a large portion of the increased payroll costs.[13]

Raising the Minimum Wage Will Provide Much-Needed Relief to American Workers

American workers desperately need—and deserve—a raise to at least $15 per hour. The current federal minimum wage is simply not enough to cover living expenses, even for a full-time worker. If the minimum wage had been adjusted automatically to reflect increases in productivity over the past 80 years, the minimum wage would now be more than $20 per hour.[14] Raising the federal minimum wage incrementally to $15 by 2025 would increase the income of 32 million workers.[15] Furthermore, establishing automatic increases to this wage tied to growth in median wages would ensure that all workers benefit from a growing economy, as well as provide a critical dampener on economic inequality.[16]

Not only would a minimum wage increase benefit millions of workers—it would also make the economy more equitable and drive growth. The workers who would benefit the most would be Black or African American, Hispanic or Latino, and Asian workers, who— thanks to a long legacy of deeply embedded structural racism—are more likely to work low-wage jobs.[17] Women, who on average make just 82 cents for every $1 the average man makes, would also receive a significant leap forward. As a result, minimum wage increases can help shrink the racial and gender wage gaps.[18] Moreover, many of these workers serve on the front lines of the battle against the coronavirus, working in grocery stores, nursing homes, and hospitals. These workers deserve a significant raise for the health risk they assume in supplying essential services.

Small Businesses Will Benefit from a $15 Minimum Wage

Small businesses can reap several benefits from a higher minimum wage that may offset the increased payroll costs. A survey from CNBC found that a majority of small businesses can absorb the rise in labor costs resulting from increases in state and local minimum wages in January 2021.[19] A growing number of business owners have recognized the benefits of paying a fair wage, paying living wages to their employees, and even supporting a national wage increase. Businesses represented by Business for a Fair Minimum Wage welcomed the wage increases that went into effect in several states at the beginning of 2021, stating in a press release, "Businesses depend on customers who make enough to buy what they are selling, from food to car repairs. Minimum wage increases will go right back into local economies, helping workers and businesses get through the pandemic and economic crisis."[20]

Increased Demand Is Good for Local Economies

One of the reasons that large job losses do not tend to accompany increases in the minimum wage is that the increase in low-wage workers' incomes generates increased spending in the local economy. The workers who would receive this wage increase are more likely to spend it than high-earning households—injecting local economies with a wave of consumer spending—to the benefit of local businesses.[21] The Economic Policy Institute found that raising the minimum wage to $15 per hour could increase a worker's annual salary by $5,100, which would likely go toward daily necessities.[22] A study by the Federal Reserve Bank of Chicago estimates that a $1 raise for a minimum wage worker translates to an additional $2,080 in consumer spending by their household over the course of a year.[23]

One of the first types of spending to increase when workers get raises is dining—an effect that will provide some relief to the struggling restaurant industry.[24] The increase of spending by low-income workers on household necessities and other consumer goods will help juice the economy and boost the revenue of small businesses. As David Cooper of the Economic Policy Institute aptly puts it, "The number one problem for businesses right now isn't excessive labor costs, it's a lack of demand."[25]

Small Businesses That Pay Living Wages Reap Significant Benefits

In addition to enjoying higher consumer demand, small businesses that adopt living wages benefit from a more productive workforce with fewer incidental payroll costs.[26]

Quite simply, employees that make a fair wage are able and willing to work harder. When workers experience less economic anxiety, they are better able to focus on their tasks. Moreover, better pay is related to better health outcomes, meaning workers take fewer sick days. It also means that employees are more invested in their work and are less likely to be late, miss a shift, or have other disciplinary problems.[27] In total, worker productivity and the quality of service increases, potentially allowing a firm to increase its prices to compensate for the higher pay.[28] For example, a study of nursing home staff performance after a minimum wage increase showed a significant increase in the quality of care received by residents.[29]

In addition to higher productivity from individual workers, small businesses benefit from lower staff turnover.[30] The time and money needed to recruit, interview, and train a new employee eats up significant resources. By some estimates, it costs about one-fifth of a worker's annual salary to replace them, and low-wage jobs such as retail and food service are among those with the highest turnover rates.[31] In the long term, raising the minimum wage will likely bring cost savings to small businesses that find it easier to retain employees after the wage increase.

Raising the Wage Would Not Significantly Increase Unemployment Levels

An exhaustive body of economic research has demonstrated that minimum wage increases do not substantially increase unemployment.[32] The most recent round of minimum wage increases was largely absorbed by small businesses that found other ways to cut costs and increase revenue. Before the pandemic, more than half of small business owners surveyed by CNBC in 2020 responded that the minimum wage increases in the states in which they operated would have no impact on their businesses.[33] The Raise the Wage Act would phase in the increase in the minimum wage to $15 by 2025, providing businesses with ample time to adjust their balance sheets accordingly. A recent study by the University of California, Berkeley, found that even sharp increases in minimum wages in low-wage areas do not result in significant job losses.[34]

Conclusion

The bottom line is that increased demand, boosted worker productivity, and reduced employee turnover balance out the increased labor costs for businesses of raising the minimum wage. The way to help struggling small businesses is not suppressing wages—it is speedily handling the pandemic and increasing federal assistance for distressed small enterprises. By raising the minimum wage to $15 per hour, Congress would ensure a faster, more equitable, and more sustainable economic recovery for all.

Endnotes

1. Heidi Shierholz, "The economy President-elect Biden is inheriting," Economic Policy Institute Working Economics Blog, January 8, 2020, available at https://www.epi.org/blog/the-economy-president-elect-biden-is-inheriting-26-8-million-workers-15-8-of-the-workforce-are-being-directly-hurt-by-the-coronavirus-crisis/.
2. Lauren Bauer, "Hungry at Thanksgiving: A Fall 2020 update on food insecurity in the US," Brookings Institution, November 23, 2020, available at https://www.brookings.edu/blog/up-front/2020/11/23/hungry-at-thanksgiving-a-fall-2020-update-on-food-insecurity-in-the-u-s/.
3. Josh Bivens and others, "Moral policy = good economics," Economic Policy Institute Working Economics Blog, October 30, 2020, available at https://www.epi.org/blog/moral-policy-good-economics-whats-needed-to-lift-up-140-million-poor-and-low-income-people-further-devastated-by-the-pandemic/; Zachary Parolin and others, "Monthly Poverty Rates in the United States during the COVID-19 Pandemic" (New York: Columbia University, 2020), available at https://static1.squarespace.com/static/5743308460b5e922a25a6dc7/t/5f87c59e4cd0011fabd38973/1602733471158/COVID-Projecting-Poverty-Monthly-CPSP-2020.pdf.
4. David Cooper, Elise Gould, and Ben Zipperer, "Low-wage workers are suffering from a decline in the real value of the federal minimum wage" (Washington: Economic Policy Institute, 2019), available at https://www.epi.org/publication/labor-day-2019-minimum-wage/; David Cooper, "Raising the federal minimum wage to $15 by 2024 would lift pay for nearly 40 million workers" (Washington: Economic Policy Institute, 2019), available at https://www.epi.org/publication/raising-the-federal-minimum-wage-to-15-by-2024-would-lift-pay-for-nearly-40-million-workers/.
5. National Low-Income Housing Coalition, "Out of Reach 2020," https://reports.nlihc.org/oor/about (last accessed February 2021).
6. US Department of Labor, "Questions and Answers About the Minimum Wage," available at https://www.dol.gov/agencies/whd/minimum-wage/faq (last accessed February 2021); Alina Selyukh, "Workers with Disabilities Can Earn Just $3.34 an Hour. Agency Says Law Needs Change," NPR, September 17, 2020, available at https://www.npr.org/2020/09/17/912840482/u-s-agency-urges-end-to-below-minimum-wage-for-workers-with-disabilities.
7. Bivens and others, "Moral policy = good economics."
8. Nick Leiber, "The Uneven Road Ahead for America's Small Businesses," Bloomberg Businessweek, February 10, 2021, available at https://www.bloomberg.com/news

/articles/2021-02-10/molly-moon-s-homemade-ice-cream-on-running-business-in-seattle-during-covid.
9. US Census Bureau, "Small Business Pulse Survey," available at https://portal.census.gov/pulse/data/ (last accessed February 2021).
10. Tina Highfall and others, "Measuring the Small Business Economy" (Washington: US Bureau of Economic Analysis, 2020), available at https://www.bea.gov/index.php/system/files/papers/BEA-WP2020-4_0.pdf.
11. Kori Hale, "Here's What the New Round of PPP Loans Means for Black-Owned Businesses," *Forbes*, January 5, 2021, available at https://www.forbes.com/sites/korihale/2021/01/05/heres-what-the-new-round-of-ppp-loans-means-for-black-owned-businesses/?sh=301f873346ee.
12. Tonya Mosley and Allison Hagan, "Small Businesses Call for Delays to Minimum Wage Increases Amid Pandemic Turmoil," WBUR, December 15, 2020, available at https://www.wbur.org/hereandnow/2020/12/15/minimum-wage-coronavirus.
13. Michael Reich, "Likely Effects of a $15 Federal Minimum Wage by 2024" (Berkeley, CA: UC Berkeley Center on Wage and Employment Dynamics, 2019), available at https://www.congress.gov/116/meeting/house/108844/witnesses/HHRG-116-ED00-Wstate-ReichM-20190207.pdf.
14. Bivens and others, "Moral policy = good economics."
15. Economic Policy Institute, "Why the US needs a $15 minimum wage" (Washington: 2021), available at https://www.epi.org/publication/why-america-needs-a-15-minimum-wage/.
16. Kate Bahn and Will McGrew, "Factsheet: Minimum wage increases are good for US workers and the US economy" (Washington: Washington Center for Equitable Growth, 2019), available at https://equitablegrowth.org/factsheet-minimum-wage-increases-are-good-for-u-s-workers-and-the-u-s-economy/.
17. Ibid.; Danyelle Solomon, Connor Maxwell, and Abril Castro, "Systemic Inequality and Economic Opportunity" (Washington: Center for American Progress, 2019), available at https://www.americanprogress.org/issues/race/reports/2019/08/07/472910/systematic-inequality-economic-opportunity/.
18. National Women's Law Center, "The Wage Gap: The Who, How, Why, and What to Do" (Washington: 2020), available at https://nwlc.org/wp-content/uploads/2019/09/Wage-Gap-Who-how.pdf.
19. Laura Wronski and Jon Cohen, "Minimum wage increases aren't a job killer: Small business survey," CNBC, February 20, 2020, available at https://www.cnbc.com/2020/02/20/minimum-wage-increases-arent-a-job-killer-small-business-survey.html.
20. Business for a Fair Minimum Wage, "Business Leaders Say New Year Minimum Wage Hikes Will Boost Consumer Spending, Help the Economy," Press release, December 28, 2020, available at https://www.businessforafairminimumwage.org/news/001614/business-leaders-say-new-year-minimum-wage-hikes-will-boost-consumer-spending-help.
21. David Cooper, "Now is still a good time to raise the minimum wage," Economic Policy Institute Working Economics Blog, June 24, 2020, available at https://www.epi.org/blog/now-is-still-a-good-time-to-raise-the-minimum-wage/.
22. Cooper, "Raising the minimum wage to $15 by 2024 would lift wages for 41 million American workers."
23. William M. Rogers III, "Making the Economic Case for a $15 Minimum Wage," The Century Foundation, January 28, 2019, available at https://tcf.org/content/commentary/making-economic-case-15-minimum-wage/?session=1; Yanney Lathrop, "Raising the Minimum Wage Leads to Significant Gains for Workers, Not

to 'Benefit Cliffs,'" (New York: National Employment Law Project, 2020), available at https://www.nelp.org/publication/raising-minimum-wage-leads-significant-gains -workers-not-benefits-cliffs/.

24. Daniel Cooper, María José Luengo-Prado, and Jonathan A. Parker, "The Local Aggregate Effects of Minimum Wage Increases" (Cambridge, MA: National Bureau of Economic Research, 2019), available at https://www.nber.org/papers/w25761?utm_ campaign=ntwh&utm_medium=email&utm_source=ntwg11; US Census Bureau, "Small Business Pulse Survey."

25. Cooper, "Now is still a good time to raise the minimum wage."

26. Laura Huizar, "A $12 Minimum Wage: Broad Benefits for Workers and Small Businesses Across Missouri" (New York: National Employment Law Project, 2018), available at https://www.nelp.org/publication/12-minimum-wage-broad-benefits-workers-small -businesses-across-missouri/; Peterson Institute for International Economics, "Raising Lower-Level Wages: When and Why It Makes Economic Sense" (Washington: 2015), available at https://piie.com/publications/briefings/piieb15-2.pdf.

27. Ibid.

28. Krista Ruffini, "Worker earnings, service quality, and firm profitability: Evidence from nursing homes and minimum wage reforms" (Washington: Washington Center for Equitable Growth, 2020), available at https://equitablegrowth.org/working-papers /worker-earnings-service-quality-and-firm-profitability-evidence-from-nursing -homes-and-minimum-wage-reforms/.

29. Ibid.; Peterson Institute for International Economics, "Raising Lower-Level Wages."

30. Kathy Eckhouse, Written testimony before the US House Committee on Education and Labor, February 7, 2019, available at https://edlabor.house.gov/imo/media/doc /Testimony_Eckhouse020719.pdf.

31. Heather Boushey and Sarah Jane Glynn, "There Are Significant Business Costs to Replacing Employees" (Washington: Center for American Progress, 2012), available at https://www.americanprogress.org/issues/economy/reports/2012/11/16/44464/there -are-significant-business-costs-to-replacing-employees/; US Bureau of Labor Statistics, "Table 16. Annual total separations rates by industry and region, not seasonally adjusted," available at https://www.bls.gov/news.release/jolts.t16.htm (last accessed February 2021).

32. Doruk Cengiz and others, "The Effect of Minimum Wages on Low-Wage Jobs," *The Quarterly Journal of Economics* 134 (3) (2019): 1405–1454, available at https:// academic.oup.com/qje/article/134/3/1405/5484905; Paul J. Wolfson and Dale Belman, "15 Years of Research on US Employment and the Minimum Wage" (Hanover, NH: Dartmouth College Tuck School of Business, 2015), available at https://papers.ssrn .com/sol3/papers.cfm?abstract_id=2705499; Reich, "Likely Effects of a $15 Federal Minimum Wage by 2024"; Bahn and McGrew, "Factsheet: Minimum wage increases are good for US workers and the US economy."

33. Wronski and Cohen, "Minimum wage increases aren't a job killer."

34. Anna Godoey and Michael Reich, "Minimum Wage Effects in Low-Wage Areas," (Berkeley, CA: UC Berkeley Institute for Research on Labor and Employment, 2019), available at https://irle.berkeley.edu/minimum-wage-effects-in-low-wage-areas/.

Periodical and Internet Sources Bibliography

The following articles have been selected to supplement the diverse views presented in this chapter.

Gabby Birenbaum, "Poll: 61% of Likely Voters Support Democrats' Gradual Minimum Wage Hike," Vox, February 24, 2021. https://www.vox.com/2021/2/24/22299029/poll-majority-support-15-minimum-wage-democrats

Brad Close, "Big Business Backs a Minimum Wage Increase Because It Would Crush Main Street Competitors," *USA Today*, February 20, 2021. https://www.usatoday.com/story/opinion/2021/02/26/big-business-behind-push-for-15-minimum-wage-column/4545386001/

William Dunkelberg, "$15 Minimum Wage Attacks on Small Businesses," *Forbes*, April 12, 2021. https://www.forbes.com/sites/williamdunkelberg/2021/04/12/15-federal-minimum-wage-attacks-on-small-businesses/?sh=46a8a87e4e21

Nicole Fallert, "CEO Who Raised Company Minimum Wage to $70,000 Says Revenue Has Tripled," *Newsweek*, April 14, 2021. https://www.newsweek.com/ceo-who-raised-company-minimum-wage-70k-says-revenue-has-tripled-1583610

Louise Matsakis, "Why Amazon Really Raised Its Minimum Wage to $15 an Hour," *Wired*, October 2, 2018. https://www.wired.com/story/why-amazon-really-raised-minimum-wage/

H. Lee Murphy, "Amazon's Giving Raises. What about You?" *Crain's Chicago Business*, July 19, 2021. https://www.chicagobusiness.com/private-intelligence/amazons-giving-raises-what-about-you

Ana Ortega, "A $15 Minimum Wage Is Needed, but Aid for Small Businesses Should Be Prioritized," *Denver University Clarion*, March 8, 2021. https://duclarion.com/2021/03/a-15-minimum-wage-is-needed-but-aid-for-small-businesses-should-be-prioritized/

Christopher Rugaber, "15 Minimum Wage Becoming Norm as Employers Struggle to Fill Jobs," Associated Press, July 27, 2021. https://apnews.com/article/business-health-coronavirus

-pandemic-minimum-wage-940a6a7530d734242c6f384b75
1b8033

Noam Scheiber, "Biden Orders $15 Minimum Wage for Federal
Contractors," *New York Times*, April 27, 2021. https://www
.nytimes.com/2021/04/27/business/economy/biden-minimum
-wage-federal-contractors.html

Joseph Semprevivo, "I Own a Small Business—This Is What a $15
Minimum Wage Means to Me," *Market Watch*, updated May 15,
2021. https://www.marketwatch.com/story/i-own-a
-small-business-this-is-what-a-15-minimum-wage-means-for
-me-11620747548

Ben Winck and Dominick Reuter, "Amazon Is Establishing a New
Minimum Wage in America," *Business Insider,* May 25, 2021.
https://www.businessinsider.com/new-minumum-wage-amazon
-salaries-worker-pay-labor-market-shortage-2021-5

CHAPTER 4

Is Raising the Minimum Wage a Moral Imperative?

Chapter Preface

So far in this volume, the viewpoints have been concerned with potential economic consequences of raising the minimum wage to $15 an hour. Will it reduce poverty? Will it harm workers? Will it destroy businesses? In this chapter, we turn to a very different and more fundamental question. Is it the right thing to do?

Is paying people a living wage for their work a moral imperative? If we are to treat people with dignity and respect, value them as human beings rather than nameless, faceless workers and automatons, are we then required to pay them fairly for the work they do?

Several of this chapter's viewpoints take the above as their starting assumption. Of course, paying a living wage is the right thing to do. These viewpoints look at the ethical benefits in terms of reducing racial and gender inequities as well as making sure that workers are paid a fair wage for their work. Some authors also offer tips and suggestions for how businesses can meet these moral obligations without damaging their bottom lines.

However, some of the authors here take a decidedly different stance. They argue that not only is an increased wage not a moral requirement, but *raising* it is in fact immoral. How could that be? Well, some authors say that business owners have a right to run their businesses how they see fit, even if this results in harm to workers. Others say that workers themselves are harmed by mandated minimum wages because they don't have the option of choosing to work for whatever pay they choose.

Some business leaders are coming to believe that a living wage (perhaps even more than $15 an hour in some cases) is the right thing to do. But perhaps just as many believe that a minimum wage restricts the freedom not only of the market, but of individual workers as well.

> *"Business leaders in tough settings
> like retail who would rather offer
> living wages than poverty-level wages
> should know that they can do so by
> redesigning their operations in a
> way that allows them to afford those
> wages without raising prices."*

Raising Wages Is the Right Thing to Do

Zeynep Ton

*In the following viewpoint, Zeynep Ton opens with an analysis of
the differences in income between what the author calls "the elite"
and the "working poor." The viewpoint then goes on to discuss how
different types of businesses might be able to absorb the costs of pay
increases if the federal minimum wage were raised. Most significantly,
however, the author argues that paying a living wage is the right
thing to do, and businesses must do the hard work necessary to make
it viable. The moral obligation to society outweighs any negatives to
businesses. Zeynep Ton is a professor at the Massachusetts Institute
of Technology Sloan School of Management and president of the
Good Jobs Institute.*

"Raising Wages Is the Right Thing to Do, and Doesn't Have to Be Bad for Your Bottom
Line," by Zeynep Ton, *Harvard Business Review*, April 18, 2019. Reprinted by permission.

As you read, consider the following questions:

1. Why, according to this viewpoint, would increasing the pay of low-wage workers not be risky for companies such as JPMorgan Chase?
2. Why are business leaders growing increasingly embarrassed by the problem of the working poor?
3. What type of leadership is required for companies to succeed while paying fair wages, according to the author?

The "working poor" are a growing problem in America—one that is increasingly embarrassing to the corporate elite. Business leaders who are morally inclined to do the right thing should and can play a stronger role in solving this problem by raising wages to a level where their employees' earnings cover the cost of living.

Jamie Dimon, CEO of JPMorgan Chase, was recently stumped in a US House Financial Services Committee hearing when California Congresswoman Katie Porter asked him what advice he could give to a constituent—one of his own bank's tellers, who makes $2,425 a month and lives with her daughter in a one-bedroom apartment with a $1,600 rent in Irvine. Food, utilities, childcare, and commuting cost about another $1,400, leaving her $567 short every month. Dimon had no good answer.

Yet Dimon is one of a number of corporate leaders—others include Warren Buffett, Ray Dalio, and Paul Tudor Jones—who have expressed public concern that the version of capitalism that has allowed them to be so successful is not sustainable for our society. The data are daunting. Between 1980 and 2014, while the pre-tax income doubled for the top 1% and tripled for the top 0.1%, there was little change for the bottom 50%. In 2017, more than 45 million Americans worked in occupations whose median wage was below $15 an hour. Although wage increases have finally been accelerating, 40% of Americans are living so close to the edge that they cannot absorb an unexpected $400 expense—not much, as car repairs or dental work go.

For business leaders operating in settings like that of JPMorgan Chase, where profit margins are high and low-wage employees are a small driver of overall costs, doing the right thing morally is not even that risky. Some wage increases would even pay themselves by increasing productivity and reducing turnover—employees would be more motivated, less distracted with life problems, and less eager to find a better job. For those leaders compelled by the same moral argument but operating in businesses with low profit margins and a high percentage of low-wage employees, doing the right thing morally is still possible. But it requires a lot more work.

When Doing the Right Thing Has Little Business Risk

During the last few years, several business leaders have substantially increased the minimum wages for their employees, citing both a moral imperative and a "business case." In 2015, Mark Bertolini, CEO of Aetna Insurance, announced a minimum wage hike from $12 an hour to $16 an hour. It wasn't right, he said, for a thriving Fortune 100 company to have employees on public assistance with their kids on Medicaid. Furthermore, he could justify "doing the right thing" economically: "Let's look at all the potential benefits we can drive, hard and soft, as a result of this investment, put some numbers on them and stand back and say, 'Is this a risk we are willing to take?'" He thought so.

And in 2016, Jamie Dimon himself announced that JPMorgan Chase would increase the minimum wage for 16,000 of its employees from $10.15 an hour to anywhere from $12 to $16 an hour, depending on where they worked. "It is the right thing to do," he said, and it would also benefit the company by attracting and retaining talent. The wage increase was significant, although it clearly didn't lift up everyone, including Rep. Porter's constituent, to a living wage.

What these examples have in common, however, is that the company could already afford the raise. JPMorgan Chase's increase affected only about 7% of its employees and the company had more than enough profit margin to afford it. So did Aetna.

When Doing the Right Thing Can Wipe Out Profits

But what happens when the company can't easily afford a significant wage increase? For some companies, a 30% raise for their lowest-wage employees, like Aetna's, could wipe out profitability, at least in the short term. Take retail, for example, the largest employer in the United States, where labor costs are around 10% of sales and the profit margins can be in single digits. Business conditions like this—high labor intensity and low profit margins—are where most of the working poor are; the 2017 median wage for the 8.7 million US retail sales workers was $10.77 an hour.

Some retail leaders would like to do better by their low-wage employees. They are also being pushed from a competitive perspective: Minimum wages are increasing, labor markets are tight, and creating a compelling customer experience requires a motivated, capable, and stable workforce. Indeed, several retailers—including Amazon, Walmart, CVS, and Target—have announced wage increases since early 2018.

But when labor intensity and profit margin seem to forbid higher wages, how can they make the moral and competitive case work financially? The way out of this trap is to design jobs in a way that increases workers' productivity and enables them to drive sales and lower costs. In short, you make it possible to pay workers more by making them worth more to your business. That, as you might surmise, requires a different leadership focus—a different view of what are the company's most valuable assets and what investments they require.

Costco, for example, can offer a $15-an-hour minimum wage and pay store employees an average of about $22 an hour with generous benefits because it has made specific operating system design choices—such as offering fewer products and promotions, setting clear standards, and empowering employees to make decisions—which enable its employees to be highly productive and to contribute significantly to customer value.

Costco's operating system also requires leadership with the following key features:

Humility—an acceptance that one cannot design everything from the top and that the best ideas to improve work come from people who do the work.

Faith in people—a deep belief that most people want to do a good job and be proud of their work.

A passion for operational excellence—to do all the mundane but important things really well. "If you are a big picture guy, you are not in the picture," Costco co-founder Jim Sinegal told my students. "Retail is detail." When he ran Costco, he spent about 200 days a year visiting stores. He focused on detail: how the products were displayed, how they were priced—always through the customers' eyes.

Business leaders in tough settings like retail who would rather offer living wages than poverty-level wages should know that they can do so by redesigning their operations in a way that allows them to afford those wages without raising prices. This is hard work and you'll have to make hard decisions. Are you the type of leader who is willing to take that on and to defend what you're doing—to your board and analysts—financially, competitively, and morally?

As for Jamie Dimon, I hope he will further evaluate wages in his company and do the right thing, even if he has to do it the hard way with better-designed jobs.

> *"During the COVID-19 pandemic,*
> *essential and front-line workers have*
> *kept the economy running at great*
> *risk to their health and their families."*

Raising the Minimum Wage Would Help Reduce Racial and Gender Inequities

David Cooper, Zane Mokhiber, and Ben Zipperer

In the following excerpted viewpoint, David Cooper, Zane Mokhiber, and Ben Zipperer look at the moral costs of poverty-level wages by focusing on racial and gender inequities in pay. The authors point out that the people being underpaid tend to do work that is important to society: child and elder care, as well as what since the pandemic we've recognized as "essential front-line work." David Cooper is a senior economic analyst at the Economic Policy Institute (EPI). Zane Mokhiber is a data analyst for EPI. Ben Zipperer is an economist with EPI.

As you read, consider the following questions:

1. How would raising the minimum wage reduce pay inequities between whites and people of color?
2. What work typically earns "poverty wages"?
3. How would the proposed minimum wage law prevent low-wage workers from slipping back into poverty?

"Raising the Federal Minimum Wage to $15 by 2025 Would Lift the Pay of 32 Million Workers," by David Cooper, Zane Mokhiber, and Ben Zipperer, Economic Policy Institute, March 9, 2021. Reprinted by permission.

The Raise the Wage Act of 2021 would help eliminate poverty-level wages by raising the national minimum wage to $15 per hour by 2025. This report finds that the raise is long overdue and would deliver broad benefits to workers and the economy.

[…]

An Increase in the National Minimum Wage Is Well Overdue

The federal minimum wage has not been raised in over a decade; it has remained stuck at $7.25 per hour since 2009. [Comparing] the trajectory of the minimum wage at face value (known in economics as the nominal minimum wage) with the inflation-adjusted or "real" value of the minimum wage (representing its purchasing power) and with the real value of the minimum wage had it risen with productivity after 1948, rising costs of living since the last increase in the nominal minimum wage in 2009 have diminished the purchasing power of the federal minimum wage, which had declined by 17% as of 2020 and 18% as of 2021, a devastating fall in the earnings of the lowest-wage workers.

With the exception of some important increases, the inflation-adjusted value of the minimum wage has mostly stagnated or declined since the 1970s. But that was not always the case: In the 1950s and 1960s, Congress raised the minimum wage more frequently such that it rose roughly in line with the pace of economywide productivity. At the peak purchasing power of the minimum wage in 1968, a minimum wage worker earned $10.59 per hour (in 2021 dollars), 46% more than a worker at the $7.25 federal minimum wage today. Had Congress continued to increase the minimum wage in line with productivity growth, the minimum wage today would be over $22 per hour. Despite the doubling of labor productivity, minimum wage workers today are paid substantially less in real terms than their counterparts earned five decades ago.

[…]

A $15 minimum wage by 2025 would disproportionately benefit Black and Hispanic workers and women, raise the pay of essential and front-line workers, and reduce the number of people living in poverty. [...]

An Increase in the National Minimum Wage Supports a More Racially Just Economy

Due to occupational segregation, discrimination, and other impacts of systemic racism, racial pay disparities are one of the persistent, structural features of the US labor market (Wilson and Rodgers 2016). Despite some historical progress, in 2019 Hispanic workers were being paid 10.8% less than white workers with similar ages and education levels, and Black workers were being paid 14.9% less than comparable white workers (Gould 2020).

Our analysis of shares of workers affected, combined with recent research on minimum wages and racial income and earnings gaps, indicates that raising the minimum wage to $15 by 2025 would substantially reduce racial pay inequality. While the raise would increase wages for less than one out of five (18.4%) white workers, about one in three (31.3%) Black workers and one in four (26.0%) Hispanic workers would receive a pay increase. Because they are particularly underpaid, women of color would disproportionately benefit from the Raise the Wage Act: 22.9% of those who would receive pay increases are Black or Hispanic women.

Ending the separate, tipped wage would especially benefit women of color, as they are more likely to work in tipped jobs and be paid subminimum wages. The National Women's Law Center (2021) finds that nearly 70% of tipped workers are women, and that Latinas and Black, Native American, and Asian American/Pacific Islander women are all disproportionately represented among tipped workers.

Civil rights leaders and advocates have long recognized the value of higher wage standards in reducing inequality. In 1963, the federal minimum wage was $1.15 an hour, and there was no minimum wage at all for agriculture, nursing homes, restaurants,

INCREASE UNEMPLOYMENT BUT
LIFT 900,000 OUT OF POVERTY

An analysis by the nonpartisan Congressional Budget Office released Monday found that the $15 federal minimum wage bill proposed by Democrats would cut jobs for 1.4 million workers by 2025, but lift 900,000 people out of poverty.

Why it matters: President Biden included a proposal to increase the minimum wage from $7.25 to $15 an hour in his $1.9 trillion coronavirus relief plan, but it's facing resistance from moderate Democrats like Sen. Joe Manchin (D-W.Va.). Biden said over the weekend that he does not expect the provision to survive negotiations, but that he'll push for it in a separate bill.

"No one should work 40 hours a week and live below the poverty wage. And if you're making less than $15 an hour, you're living below the poverty wage," Biden said.

Details: The CBO report found that a $15 minimum wage phase-in by June 2025, as proposed by Democrats, would have the following effects:

• Increase the cumulative budget deficit over the 2021–2031 period by $54 billion.
• Drive prices higher for goods and services—"stemming from the higher wages of workers paid at or near the minimum wage."

and other service industries that disproportionately employed Black workers. The 1963 March on Washington for Jobs and Freedom (the March on Washington) called for a $2.00 minimum wage (Pitts and Allegretto 2013). As Derenoncourt (2020) has observed, the 1963 March on Washington's demand would be equivalent to about $15.00 today after adjusting for inflation.

The 1963 March on Washington demanded a $2.00 minimum wage that would "include all areas of employment which are presently excluded" and would "give all Americans a decent standard of living" (Derenoncourt 2020).

- Increase wages for 17 million workers who currently make under $15 an hour, as well as 10 million workers whose wages would otherwise be slightly above that wage rate.
- The cumulative pay of affected people would "increase, on net, by $333 billion."
- That net increase would come from "higher pay ($509 billion) for people who were employed at higher hourly wages under the bill, offset by lower pay ($175 billion) because of reduced employment under the bill," the report adds.

Context: The CBO is a nonpartisan federal agency that analyzes the effects of proposed fiscal policies.

What they're saying: Senate Budget Committee Chair Bernie Sanders wrote in response on Monday, "I find it hard to understand how the CBO concluded that raising the minimum wage would increase the deficit by $54 billion. Two years ago, CBO concluded that a $15 minimum wage would increase the deficit by less than $1 million over ten years."

"The good news, however, is that from a Byrd Rule perspective, the CBO has demonstrated that increasing the minimum wage would have a direct and substantial impact on the federal budget," he added.

"What that means is that we can clearly raise the minimum wage to $15 an hour under the rules of reconciliation."

"CBO: $15 Minimum Wage Would Increase Unemployment but Lift 900,000 Out of Poverty," by Ursula Perano, Axios, February 8, 2021.

Several years later, Congress expanded the coverage of the minimum wage and eventually raised it to its historical high point of $1.60 in 1968, or $10.59 in 2021 dollars. Derenoncourt and Montialoux (2021) describe how the new standard raised wages overall but had its largest effects on Black workers. Just before the increase, 28.8% of Black workers earned at or below the 1967 minimum, compared with 13.9% of white workers. The authors convincingly demonstrate that these increases were responsible for more than 20% of the fall in the Black–white earnings gap during the Civil Rights Era. Since then, minimum wages have continued to play a substantial role in reducing racial earnings inequality. Wursten and Reich (2021) found that minimum wage increases between 1990 and 2019 reduced Black–white wage gaps by 12% overall, and by 60% for workers with only a high school diploma or less. The link between increases in the minimum wage and decreases in racial earnings gaps also means that the erosion of the federal minimum wage over this period increased racial earnings gaps.

Essential and Front-Line Workers Constitute a Majority of Those Who Would See Pay Raises by Raising the Minimum Wage to $15

During the COVID-19 pandemic, essential and front-line workers have kept the economy running at great risk to their health and their families. The US labor market, however, has not fairly rewarded that vital work. Very few essential workers receive hazard pay to compensate for their now-more dangerous work, and low pay among essential and front-line workers continues to be pervasive (Dorman and Mishel 2020; McNicholas and Poydock 2020). Kinder and Stateler (2021) found that in 2018, essential workers made up nearly half (22.3 million) of the 47.7 million US workers in occupations in which the median wage was less than $15 per hour. In our analysis, we find that a majority of workers who would benefit from the Raise the Wage Act are essential or front-line workers.

[…]

Poverty Would Decrease and Economic Security Would Increase Under a $15 Minimum Wage

The five-decade decline and stagnation of the minimum wage has prevented millions of people, often children, from maintaining an adequate standard of living. Notably among minimum wage workers struggling to get by are those whose incomes are so low they fall under the federal poverty threshold.

From its origins, the minimum wage has been an important policy tool in the fight against poverty. The Fair Labor Standards Act was enacted in 1938 "to protect this Nation from the evils and dangers resulting from wages too low to buy the bare necessities of life."[3] Thirty years later, higher wages were one of five key demands of the Economic Bill of Rights of the 1968 Poor People's Campaign (Johnson 2018).

Unfortunately, infrequent and inadequate increases in the national minimum have reduced it to a poverty wage. A full-time minimum wage worker in 1968 would have earned roughly $22,000 a year (in 2021 dollars), but today their counterpart could earn only about $15,000 working full time. As a consequence, a single parent working full time would be in poverty if they earned the federal minimum wage and had no other source of income.

[…]

A $15 Minimum Wage Would Advance Gender Justice

In addition to the disproportionate impact that it would have for workers of color and those in essential and front-line jobs, raising the federal minimum wage would broadly benefit women workers. A $15 minimum wage in 2025 would provide a pay raise to nearly 19 million women—roughly one in four women workers in the United States. Women make up nearly 60% of all those who would benefit from the policy.

[…]

Conclusion

The Raise the Wage Act charts the path forward to where we, as a society, should target a minimum wage in 2025. Raising the federal minimum wage to $15 by 2025 would secure a long-overdue improvement in living standards for the lowest-wage workers and will finally help ensure that full-time work is a means to escape poverty. The policy would significantly reduce long-standing race- and gender-based pay inequities and the inequities between how tipped and nontipped workers are treated. Finally, by automatically linking future increases to median wage growth, it will prevent those with the lowest pay from slipping behind.

Endnotes

3. S. Rep. No. 75-884, at 4 (1937).

> *"Any positive or negative outcomes are not for 'the economy' as such, only for people. And the people in the economy are all of us, including the illegal immigrants."*

To Reduce Harm to Low-Wage Undocumented Immigrants, Don't Raise Wages, Open the Borders

Howard Baetjer

This historical viewpoint was written by Howard Baetjer in 2007, when Congress was discussing the last minimum wage increase. After making familiar claims about the harm an increase would do to both businesses and workers, the author turns to an issue still pertinent today: illegal immigration. Baetjer argues that raising the minimum wage would cause businesses to hire more illegal immigrants, who would often still choose to do less valuable work to reduce the chances of being deported. The solution, he says, is not a higher minimum wage, but open borders. Howard Baetjer is a lecturer in economics at Towson University in Towson, Maryland.

"At the Intersection of the Minimum Wage and Illegal Immigration," by Howard Baetjer, Foundation for Economic Education, March 1, 2007. https://fee.org/articles/at-the -intersection-of-the-minimum-wage-and-illegal-immigration/. Licensed under CC BY- ND-4.0.

As you read, consider the following questions:

1. What does the author mean when he says outcomes of raising the minimum wage are not for "the economy," but for people?
2. Why, according to the viewpoint, do undocumented immigrants sometimes prefer to work for lower wages than others might?
3. What is Baetjer's solution to the problem of illegal immigration?

This question from a former student named Blake addresses the interaction of two hot political issues: "I remember in class that raising minimum wage is a bad thing to do. My question to you is, since illegal immigrants don't get paid minimum wage most of the time, does that aid in bringing down wages and creating a positive outcome for the economy?"

My answer was an uneasy yes and no. Any positive or negative outcomes are not for "the economy" as such, only for people. And the people in the economy are all of us, including the illegal immigrants. Illegal immigration may reduce the overall harm done by increases in the minimum wage, but better all around would be legal immigration and no minimum wage. Let's sort the issues out to see why.

First, Blake is correct that "raising minimum wage is a bad thing to do" because it does most harm to the least-advantaged among us. The benefits of a higher minimum wage are much easier to perceive than the harms. The benefits go to all workers who keep their jobs when the minimum is raised (without losing enough hours' work to decrease their incomes). They get a pay raise. These are the benefits that minimum-wage advocates focus on.

The harm done by the minimum wage is harder to perceive. The key to understanding it is the insight that nobody will pay an employee more than that employee's value to the business, at least not for long. If you are the employer and you believe that a low-skilled young person contributes about $6 of value to your company every hour, you'll be willing to pay that person up to $6 an hour. If an increase in the minimum wage then forces you to raise his pay to $7 an hour, you'll lose a dollar an hour if you keep him on. You'll have to lay him off.

Minimum-wage laws that force wages above the rates that would be freely negotiated in the market throw people out of work. This is a fundamental conclusion of economic reasoning, supported by the vast majority of scholarly studies of the minimum wage.

What kinds of workers, exactly, get thrown out of work? Suppose you employ a number of low-skilled young people at $5.15 an hour at your fast-food restaurant along with your higher-skilled managers. Some of these minimum-wage workers are more skilled, more responsible, or more experienced than others. Now suppose the minimum wage is raised to $7.25 an hour (as is being discussed in Congress as of this writing). Suppose you calculate that the higher wage rates you now must pay will make it unprofitable for you to keep your restaurant open during the same hours at the same prices. You'll have to either raise prices or shut down at the least-busy times of day, or some combination of the two. Whatever course you take, you'll reduce the number of hours' work for your employees. If you raise prices, you won't have as many customers, so you'll need fewer workers to serve them. If you reduce your hours of operation, you won't need your workers for as long.

Whose hours will you cut back? Those of the more-skilled, more-responsible, more-experienced workers? Probably not. You will cut back on the hours of, or perhaps lay off altogether, the least-skilled, least-responsible, least-experienced workers. Those who will have the hardest time getting another job, those who most urgently need the experience of an entry-level job, are the ones who get laid off.

Who else is harmed by the minimum wage? In our example, your managers and other more-skilled workers are also harmed by having their hours cut back. Unlike the least-skilled workers who have nowhere else to go when they lose their entry-level jobs, the more-skilled workers can find work elsewhere. But when they do, it will be at jobs that don't pay quite so well or otherwise are not as attractive to them—or else they would have chosen to work there instead of at your restaurant in the first place. Thus these workers are hurt even if they keep the same number of work hours.

While some workers lose their jobs (or enough hours of work to reduce their total incomes), other workers get paid more. We can't know which effect is greater without unknowable details about the lives and values of the different workers. But clearly the law harms the most disadvantaged—the very workers that minimum-wage advocates claim to want to help. This is the overlooked human tragedy of the minimum wage.

What about consumers (who are rarely considered in public commentary on the minimum wage)? Consumers who would like to eat at your restaurant during off-hours are harmed because now you are closed at those times. If you stay open the same hours but charge higher prices, consumers are hurt by the added expense. The output of your laid-off workers is denied them, and the output of the higher-skilled workers and managers driven into other work elsewhere is not worth as much to consumers as the lost output of your restaurant would have been—that's why the wages paid in those alternative jobs are lower than at your restaurant.

Here is the clear harm done to "the economy"—the people in society—taken as a whole: Because of the legal minimum wage (or its increase) valuable productive resources are forced into idleness. In our example, lower-skilled workers, better-skilled managers, the restaurant, and its equipment are all idled (or, in the case of your managers, diverted to less-valuable production), even though workers, owners, and customers all would prefer that those resources be at work in your restaurant. Productive effort and mutually beneficial exchanges that would have occurred don't occur. Society overall is poorer as a result.

Illegal Immigration's Effects

How might illegal immigration reduce this harm?

Some immigrants, here illegally to begin with, are also willing to work for illegally low wages. When they do, they help produce goods and services that would otherwise go unproduced, or be produced only at greater cost. Their willingness to work for below-minimum wages thus reduces costs and increases output for consumers. This is probably what Blake had in mind when he referred to illegal immigration "bringing down wages and creating a positive outcome for the economy." In our example, after the legal minimum wage is raised, you might be able to find illegal immigrants willing to work for less than the minimum. If so, you will be able to keep your prices down and/or stay open later in the evening. Your store, equipment, and workers would stay in productive use; consumers would benefit.

But not everything about this scenario is positive even if illegal immigration does keep actual wages and costs down closer to an appropriate, market-determined level. In certain cases it would be better still for "the economy"—for the people in the economy—to have certain illegal immigrants paid higher wages than they would receive while immigration is illegal.

Some illegal immigrants who would earn higher wages in a free labor market find themselves trapped in jobs that pay below minimum wage. Why? Because they are afraid that if they leave those jobs for others that pay more, they might be reported and thrown out of the country. This hurts consumers: it would be better to have those immigrants working at the higher-paying jobs instead, because the output of those jobs is more valuable to consumers. Let us imagine, for example, a talented carpenter who can find little work in his own country—let's call him Juan. Suppose Juan sneaks across the border, or gets himself smuggled into the United States, to work as a manual laborer at a landscaping company for below minimum wage. Though it is not much to us, that wage is much higher than he can earn in his home country.

Now suppose that a local carpenter needs an assistant whom he would pay $15–20 an hour. Juan's greatest value in the economy would then be to work as the carpenter's assistant. This is clear because the local carpenter's willingness to pay him $15 or more an hour shows that people in the community value at that amount the carpentry Juan might do each hour. For Juan's manual labor, by contrast, people are willing to pay only $6 or $7 an hour. Juan is worth more in the economy as a carpenter.

Nevertheless, when immigration is illegal Juan might well choose to do the less-valuable work because he is afraid of being deported. Perhaps the man who smuggled him in has an agreement with the head of the landscaping company and Juan worries that if he moves to a better job the smuggler might report him. Or he might worry that working as a carpenter's assistant would put him at risk of being turned in by other carpenters who would resent his competition. Or the state might require a license for carpenter's assistants, for which only legal immigrants may apply.

For these kinds of reasons illegal immigrants often hold jobs in which their work is less valuable than elsewhere. All such cases represent a clear loss to society because even though the illegal immigrants' willingness to work for below minimum wage keeps wages and costs down in the markets for lower-skilled labor, their talents are sadly wasted. They would be better used providing services that people in the community value more.

Reducing Production

Just as minimum-wage laws reduce society's overall wealth by decreasing the production of valuable goods and services, so also do laws hindering immigration. Both interfere with the labor market's essential function of directing human talent—what the late, great economist Julian Simon called "the ultimate resource"—to their most valued uses.

In answer to Blake, then, yes, it may be that illegal immigration helps to reduce the damage done by minimum-wage laws and minimum-wage increases. But no, it is incorrect to think that illegal immigration as such is beneficial for the economy. It is better than no immigration at all, but compared to free immigration, it is worse.

The problem with illegal immigration is not that it's immigration, but that it's illegal. The proper immigration policy for a free and prosperous nation is open borders—free immigration for all people who will live and work peacefully. Liberty, including liberty to move peacefully about the planet, cannot justly be infringed. It is a basic human right, and it promotes economic well-being.

> "Rather than the fruits of a successful
> business being shared with the people
> who make that business run on a
> daily basis, these companies are
> concentrating their profits in the
> hands of a few."

Raising the Wage Is a Moral Imperative

Megan Ellyia Green

In the following viewpoint, Megan Ellyia Green chronicles a 2015 consideration by the city of St. Louis to raise the local minimum wage to $13 per hour by 2020. Although the author makes a strong case about the economic reasons for raising the wage, Green also says the issue is more than economic; it is a moral imperative. Megan Ellyia Green is a member of the St. Louis Board of Aldermen and has a long history of working in the educational and nonprofit sector.

As you read, consider the following questions:

1. What is HB722?
2. Does the author ever directly address the moral question? If so, when?
3. What assumptions does Green make in her moral argument? Do you agree with those assumptions?

W hich side are you on? That's the question that must be asked when talking about St. Louis City's proposal to raise the minimum wage to $13 per hour by 2020. There are both moral and economic imperatives for raising the minimum wage. We must exercise the political courage to do so NOW.

Just in the past year, as income inequality becomes a mainstream terminology, multiple cities across the country, including Kansas City, have chosen to raise the minimum wage. At the same time, study after study has been released about the fact that 40% of children in the City of St. Louis live in poverty, and we are in the top five cities in the nation with the worst income disparity between African Americans and Caucausians. Day after day for nearly a year our most disenfranchised have taken to the streets asking government to work FOR them. We NOW have an opportunity to answer their requests.

And we must answer them NOW. With the passage of HB 722 by the Missouri General Assembly, as a City we must pass a minimum wage bill by August 28th or risk being prohibited from instituting a wage increase. St. Louis has led the State of Missouri in passing marriage equality, the smoking ban, and ban the box. Once again it is time for St. Louis to lead.

The Moral Argument

The Center on Poverty and Inequality at Georgetown Law argues that there are strong civil rights and human rights arguments for raising the minimum wage. To understand these moral arguments for #RaiseTheWage we must first confront some disconcerting facts about our present condition.

The Face of St Louis' Low-Wage Workers

Working full-time, a minimum wage worker makes $290 per week or about $15,000 per year. Contrary to popular belief, teenagers are not the bulk of low-wage workers. Rather the median age of of a person making the minimum wage in the City of St. Louis is 32. The faces of St. Louis' working poor include restaurant workers, home healthcare workers, early childhood educators, adjunct professors, nursing home employees... whose work provides value to our community and needs to be valued by our community.

Of all of the low-wage workers in the City of St. Louis, 56% are women. Forty-one percent of all African American workers and 44% of all African American females in the City of St. Louis are low-wage workers. Forty-five percent are single mothers. At the same time, the *Washington Post* reports that a person would need to make $14.52 per hour to rent a decent apartment in Missouri, meaning we have a significant portion of our population who can't even afford basic living accommodations with our current wages.

Raising the minimum wage in St. Louis to a living wage has the possibility of bringing nearly 80,000 people out of poverty.

The Role of Corporations

While workers are suffering low, stagnating, or decreasing wages, corporations are celebrating the highest profits in 85 years and CEO pay has reached an all time high. At the same time, worker productivity has increased dramatically. In fact, the national minimum wage would be $21.72 if wages had kept pace with the increases in worker productivity we have seen since the 1960s.

Rather than the fruits of a successful business being shared with the people who make that business run on a daily basis, these companies are concentrating their profits in the hands of a few. These companies are having their cake and eating it too, while leaving workers to fight over the crumbs.

We have a moral imperative to correct this course.

There are only so many private jets, houses, and fancy dinners that those at the top can buy. This concentration of wealth sits rather than stimulating the economy through consumer spending. The social costs of not paying living wages are passed along to tax-payers. In fact, Missouri taxpayers are subsidizing these profitable corporations to the tune of $644 million per year for public assistance for working families.

The Economic Argument

This is where the economic case comes in. Raising the minimum wage to $13 an hour will still not produce wealthy Americans by any means, but it will put money into the hands of consumers who will put nearly 100% of those new earnings into the economy. The Center for American Progress cites that:

> Increasing the minimum wage would put money into the pockets of low-income workers, who are likely to spend it immediately on things like housing, food, and cars. This boost in demand for goods and services helps stimulated the economy. The money gets funded back to employers who can then reinvest it in jobs and the economy.

Raising the Wage as Economic Stimulus

Raising the minimum wage is actually a vehicle to stimulate our economy. A 2011 study from the Chicago Central Reserve Bank found that for every dollar increase for a minimum wage worker there is $2,800 in new consumer spending generated by his or her household over the following year. Consumer spending drives 70% of the economy. Polls over the past year by the National Federation of Independent Business (NFIB)—a perennial opponent of minimum wage increases—have confirmed that business owners consistently identify weak sales, not labor costs, as the top problem facing their businesses.

And Speaking of Labor Costs…

Raising the minimum wage does not actually increase labor costs as much as you might think. Labor costs generally account for about 10% of the costs to run a business. Raising the minimum wage also reduces turnover and increases productivity.

But Won't This Hurt Small Business?

The vast majority of low-wage workers are employed by large highly profitable corporations, not small businesses. The Department of Labor even finds that 3 out of 5 small business owners support raising the minimum wage.

These large profitable corporations have a choice when they make their budgets each year. A budget reflects the priorities of a company. Companies like Ikea, Trader Joe's, QuikTrip and CostCo have made the choice to invest in their workers, and their businesses are gowing. Again, higher wages yield higher consuming spending, which will be inevitability be spent at small businesses.

But We're Unique. Won't Businesses Leave the City if the County Doesn't Do It?

Although St. Louis is unique in that it is an Independent City, in many cases where cities have raised the minimum wage they have done so without the entire County also raising the wage, or without the neighboring county to the city raising the wage. Of studies conducted on 288 contiguous counties with differing minimum wages no discernible impact was found on unemployment rates or result in the flight of businesses across borders. In Santa Fe, in particular, there was an 84.5% minimum wage increase from 2003 to 2007, which was found to produce no effect on employment in spite of neighboring Albuquerque not implementing a minimum wage increase until 2007.

It's Time to Pick Sides

Tuesday will be the day for Aldermen to answer, Which side are you on? It's time to choose workers over corporations. It's time to have political courage. It's time to give St. Louis a raise.

On Tuesday, I will be standing with workers.

"Essential to human freedom is the liberty for each individual to say 'yes' or 'no' to an offer made by another concerning some potential association, interaction, or exchange among two or more persons."

The Minimum Wage Is Anti-Freedom

Richard M. Ebeling

Several of the viewpoints in this volume that are opposed to a minimum wage increase are based on libertarian philosophy. In the following viewpoint, Richard M. Ebeling makes that point up front. The minimum wage, this author argues, is wrong because it denies people—both workers and employers—the freedom to make their own decisions. Richard M. Ebeling is an American libertarian economist and former president of the Foundation for Economic Education.

As you read, consider the following questions:

1. In what way are minimum wage laws paternalistic?
2. Is the right to reject an offer of employment a meaningful right when there are no other options for survival?
3. Is there a distinction between "people" and "politicians"?

"The Minimum Wage Harms Workers and Is Anti-Freedom," by Richard M. Ebeling, Foundation for Economic Education, February 17, 2018. https://fee.org/articles/the-minimum-wage-harms-workers-and-is-anti-freedom/. Licensed under CC BY-ND-4.0 International.

Most of us both value and take for granted the ability to make decisions about our own lives. When busybodies put their noses into our personal affairs, we often say, or at least think, "Mind your own business!" And yet, we live in a world in which government won't leave us alone, and instead, very actively tries to mind our business for us.

Take, for example, the legal hourly minimum wage. The federal government began dictating the minimum lawful amount an employer must pay someone working for them in 1933, as part of Franklin Roosevelt's New Deal legislation. It was declared unconstitutional in 1935 by the US Supreme Court, but was reinstituted in 1938 as part of the Fair Labor Standard Act, and the Supreme Court upheld it in a 1941 decision.

The Minimum Wage vs. Personal Choice

When first implemented, the federal hourly minimum wage was set at 25 cents/hour. Today, it ranges at $7.25/hour. But, in recent years, there has been a call to significantly increase it to as much as $15/hour. A variety of cities around the country have, in fact, instituted such legislation within their jurisdictions, with a number of state governments proposing increases in that direction within their respective boundaries.

The assertion is made that anything less than an hourly wage in that general amount (or more!) is denying a person the chance to earn a "living wage." It is offered as paternalistic intervention in the labor market, meant to improve the working and living conditions of those who may be unskilled or poorly experienced to have a chance to earn enough to get ahead in life.

Who, after all, can be against someone having some minimal amount to live decently? Only the cold, callous, and uncaring, surely; or those who are apologists and accomplices of the greedy, selfish, and profit-hungry businessmen who have no sense of humanity for those who are in their employ. That's why there needs to be a law.

Left rarely asked and less often answered is, who is the government or those behind such legislation to tell people at what hourly pay they may work in the marketplace and how much an employer is required to pay them? Essential to human freedom is the liberty for each individual to say "yes" or "no" to an offer made by another concerning some potential association, interaction, or exchange among two or more persons.

Forcing or Prohibiting Exchange

Suppose I go into a shoe store and, after looking around and trying on a few pairs, I decide to leave the store empty-handed because the store does not have the styles or the fit I'm interested in, or because the shoes are not offered at prices that seem worth paying. But suppose, now, that a large gruff fellow stands in the doorway, and declares, "The boss says that you can't leave 'til you buy shoes at the price he says you gotta pay."

I think most of us would consider this to be outrageous and unethical. Most of us would no doubt say to ourselves, who is this guy or his boss to tell me what shoes I have to buy, and at a price that I consider to be more than those shoes are worth to me, or which is beyond what my budget can afford?

Suppose, then, that the bouncer replies to any such remark you might make by saying, "Unless you buy a pair of shoes at this minimum price, then the boss says he can't afford to pay me and the other employees a 'living wage.' Buy shoes here—or else." Many of us might try to pull out our cell phones and dial 911 for police assistance.

We take it for granted that no one, regardless of the rationale, should be able to force us into an exchange or a relationship not of our own choosing and voluntary consent. Otherwise, we are a victim—a slave—to the other person's wants and wishes, at our coerced expense.

We would also be much aggrieved if there was a mutually agreeable association or exchange opportunity we did want to enter into, but someone comes along and tells us that we can't, even if that association or exchange didn't physically harm or defraud anyone else in the process.

Yet, this is precisely what government-mandated minimum wage laws demand of market participants in American society. What are some of the consequences from government-legislated minimum wage intervention into the marketplace?

The Minimum Wage and Low Skilled Unemployment

First, it results in preventing some who might have found acceptable and gainful employment from doing so. This is especially true of the unskilled and workplace inexperienced in the labor force. The only source of revenues from which an employer can pay salaries to all those he may employ is from producing, marketing, and selling a product to willing consumers at a price they are willing to pay for what he is offering for sale.

The employer, therefore, must ask himself if an existing or a prospective employee would contribute a value-added to his production process. But more importantly, will it be a value-added that is less or more than the value of the finished product said employee may assist in manufacturing? All of us like to get a bargain (paying less for something than we think it is worth to ourselves), but we never intentionally pay more for something than what we prospectively consider it to be worth. A worker whose value-added comes out as more than the value of the finished product will be paid for his hire by the employer.

When the government imposes a legal minimum hourly wage above the wage currently prevailing for various types of labor services, the law necessarily threatens the employment of any and all workers whose estimated value-added is now less than the mandated legal minimum wage.

Suppose that a worker helps to produce an addition to marketable output that has a competitive value of, say, $5 an hour. But the government has now imposed a minimum wage of $7.25/hour. Those workers whose value-added is only $5 an hour will find themselves priced out of the market: From the employer's perspective, they cost more to employ than they're worth in terms of value-adding revenue to be earned from their hire at a minimum wage of $7.25. A private enterpriser cannot successfully maintain or establish a profitable competitive edge in the long run, if (at the margin) he has to pay $7.25 for what has had, up until now, a market worth of $5.

The Minimum Wage vs. Earned Labor Skills

But the harm runs deeper for the employee, who either loses his job due to the legal minimum wage or who, to begin with, never gets a job due to the law. The lowest earners in the labor market are usually those with the least skills and work experience. That is why their productive worth is at the lower end of the wage scale.

But how can they ever acquire the on-the-job training, experience, and workplace skills if the minimum wage so prices them out of the market? Priced out, they may never have the opportunity to get their foot on the bottom or lower rungs of "the ladder of success." By being priced out of the market in this way due to minimum wage legislation, some of them may be condemned to permanent unemployment.

In this day-and-age of the modern redistributive—welfare—state, such persistent unemployment, due to the minimum wage, means that those who are gainfully employed find themselves taxed even more than would otherwise have been the case. Their salaries must provide the needed government tax revenues to cover the income transfer costs that the welfare system is expected to incur to meet the "needs" of those the government's own minimum wage policy has forced into and left in the rolls of the unemployed.

Minimum Wage Laws and the Black Market

An additional, unintended consequence is that those thus left in the limbo land of unemployment but who wish to make more money than what the welfare state redistributes to them, will turn to alternative lines of work: the underground and black market economies. Both are market economies, but the underground economy is often the arena in which income may be earned away from the prying eyes of the tax-collectors, even though the type of product or service offered for cash is completely legal. It just usually has less of a paper trail for the taxing authorities to follow.

The black market usually connotes goods or services that are legally prohibited by the government from being openly produced, sold, and used, such as narcotics and other drugs, prostitution, and various forms of gambling. While both underground and black markets have their seamier sides, especially the trade in prohibited, heavily restricted, or controlled products tend to attract market participants of a violent, cruel, and deadly type. Thus, some individuals thrown into unemployment due to the minimum wage are drawn into arenas of crime, corruption, and thuggish coercion to earn a livable income. This is an outcome, surely, that few who campaigned for minimum wage laws originally had in mind.

Who Decides Wages: People or Politicians?

But, behind all of these negative and usually unintended consequences of imposing a government-enforced hourly minimum wage, remains the fundamental ethical issue: who shall have the right to decide the terms and conditions people will have to enter gainful employment? Shall it be the individuals who are directly affected by these laws who decide what an acceptable wage is, given their own skill set and the market opportunities they find? Shall it be the prospective employers who offer work to others based on their market-based estimate of the potential value-added of a possible employee?

Or shall it be the politicians and bureaucrats, pressured by various interest groups with their own motives for asserting a right to dictate and determine the wage at which individuals who they personally know nothing about will be allowed to find a job? There is an inescapable arrogance, a hubris, on the part of those who claim to know what a person is worth in the marketplace and the wage at which he may or may not be hired.

In this the political paternalists who insist on setting minimum wages through government command and control closely resemble the socialist central planners of the twentieth century. They suffer from that same "pretense of knowledge" that F. A. Hayek criticized nearly 45 years ago in his Nobel lecture. They suffer from the dangerous delusion that they possess enough wisdom to know better than people how they should live and work, and the terms under which they may contract and exchange for mutual gain.

Freedom requires that every individual have the liberty to peacefully decide how best to direct and plan his own life and in voluntary association with others in the various corners of society. They are not free when the government can interpose itself and dictate the wage at which a human being may offer his labor services and another may choose to employ him. Anything less makes everyone an economic victim and tool of the coercing control of those commanding the halls of government.

Periodical and Internet Sources Bibliography

The following articles have been selected to supplement the diverse views presented in this chapter.

Ari Armstrong, "Minimum Wage Laws: Immoral, Crippling, and Nevertheless Supported by Many," *Objective Standard*, September 18, 2013. https://theobjectivestandard.com/2013/09/minimum-wage-laws-immoral-crippling-and-nevertheless-supported-by-many/

Andrei Cherny, "Why I Raised My Company's Minimum Wage to $25 an Hour," *Fortune*, June 11, 2021. https://fortune.com/2021/06/11/minimum-wage-25-an-hour-aspiration-ceo/

Joseph Chuman, "A Livable Wage and Human Dignity," The Hill, March 27, 2021. https://thehill.com/opinion/finance/545226-a-livable-wage-and-human-dignity

Ariel Felton, "What's 'Southern Hospitality' Without a Living Wage?" *New York Times*, February 26, 2021. https://www.nytimes.com/2021/02/26/opinion/minimum-wage-2021-georgia.html

Jack Jenkins, "Real Family Values: Raising the Federal Minimum Wage," Center for American Progress, December 10, 2013. https://www.americanprogress.org/issues/religion/reports/2013/12/10/80780/real-family-values-raising-the-federal-minimum-wage/

Greg Kaufmann, "Poor People Need a Higher Wage Not a Lesson in Morality," Talk Poverty, April 27, 2015. https://talkpoverty.org/2015/04/27/poor-people-need-higher-wage-not-lesson-morality/

Russell Meyer, "Raising Florida's Minimum Wage Is the Christian Thing to Do," *Tampa Bay Times*, September 22, 2020. https://www.tampabay.com/opinion/2020/09/22/raising-floridas-minimum-wage-is-the-christian-thing-to-do-column/

Steven Mintz, "Minimum Wage Hike Is a Moral Issue," *Pacific Coast Business Times*, April 8, 2016. https://www.pacbiztimes.com/2016/04/08/minimum-wage-hike-a-moral-issue/

News Staff, "St. Peter's Says $15 Minimum Wage Fits 'Moral Obligations,'" *Times Union*, June 18, 2021. https://www

.timesunion.com/news/article/St-Peter-s-says-15-minimum
-wage-fits-with-16258262.php

Norm Ornstein, "The Moral and Economic Imperative to Raise the
Minimum Wage," *The Atlantic*, December 4, 2013. https://www
.theatlantic.com/politics/archive/2013/12/the-moral-and
-economic-imperative-to-raise-the-minimum-wage/282064/

Jason Russell, "The Moral Case Against a $15 Minimum Wage,"
Washington Examiner, March 31, 2016. https://www
.washingtonexaminer.com/the-moral-case-against-a-15
-minimum-wage

Emily Stewart, "Life on the Minimum Wage: I Don't Expect to Be
Rich, I Just Expect to Pay the Heat Bill," Vox, April 7, 2021.
https://www.vox.com/policy-and-politics/22364633/federal
-minimum-wage-workers

Tim Worstall, "The Moral Case Against Raising the Minimum Wage,"
Forbes, March 6, 2014. https://www.forbes.com/sites
/timworstall/2014/03/06/the-moral-case-against-raising-the
-minimum-wage/?sh=664384f47df8

For Further Discussion

Chapter 1

1. In viewpoint 4, the author argues that most minimum wage employers are small "mom and pop" businesses. But large chains such as McDonald's actually employ the bulk of minimum-wage workers. How does this distinction affect the discussion of increasing minimum wages?
2. Viewpoint 4 also cites data showing that a 10 percent increase in required starting wages raises the price of burgers and pizza by about 1 percent. Yet it says that the increase in price "negates" the wage increase. How can this be? What other factors should be considered in making a calculation about how price increases affect workers?

Chapter 2

1. Isabel Soto suggests that a federally mandated $15 minimum wage would disproportionately harm Black and Hispanic workers. In what ways could that damage could be mitigated?
2. One author argues that "the law of demand" will ensure that an increased minimum wage will result in fewer jobs. However, a viewpoint in chapter 1 points out that restaurants will find ways to compensate for higher wages. How do you think the law of supply and demand would play out in this situation? What factors affect the law of supply and demand?

Chapter 3

1. How can increased technology in the workplace benefit employers? How can it benefit workers?
2. Are low-skill and unskilled workers a liability to businesses? Would such laborers be less of a liability if they were paid more? Explain your argument based on information from viewpoints in this chapter.

Chapter 4

1. Megan Ellyia Green opens her essay with the question, "Which side are you on?" *Which Side Are You On* is a popular labor song. The song and the phrase are often used by labor organizers. Why do you think Green chose this for the opening of her essay?

2. The authors in this chapter make a lot of claims about what is "moral" or "right." That is very different from the data-driven claims (no matter how problematic) made in other chapters. What does it take to make a moral argument? Do you think there are any moral arguments to be made either for or against a living wage?

Organizations to Contact

The editors have compiled the following list of organizations concerned with the issues debated in this book. The descriptions are derived from materials provided by the organizations. All have publications or information available for interested readers. The list was compiled on the date of publication of the present volume; the information provided here may change. Be aware that many organizations take several weeks or longer to respond to inquiries, so allow as much time as possible.

Campaign for America's Future

1825 K Street NW
Suite 400
Washington, DC 20006
(202) 955-5665
email: contact via website form
website: ourfuture.org

Campaign for America's Future proposes and promotes new ideas that will address the nation's pressing economic and social problems.

FairShare

218 D Street SE, #205
Washington, DC 20003
(202) 461-2472 or (202) 461-3847
email: info@fairshareonline.org
website: fairshare.org

FairShare uses social and economic justice campaigns to work for an America where everyone plays by the same rules.

Fight for Fifteen

email: info@fightfor15.org
website: fightfor15.org

The Fight for Fifteen is a global movement of fast-food workers, home health aides, child carers, teachers, airport workers, adjunct professors, retail employees, and underpaid workers everywhere demanding to be paid a living wage for their work.

Let Justice Roll Living Wage Campaign

PO Box 2441
Little Rock, AR 72203
(501) 626-9220
email: contact via website form
website: letjusticeroll.org

A leading faith, community, labor, and business coalition, Let Justice Roll is committed to raising the minimum wage to a living wage at the state and federal level.

Minority Business Development Agency

US Department of Commerce
1401 Constitution Avenue NW
Washington, DC 20230
(202) 482-2332
email: contact via website form
website: mbda.gov

A part of the US Department of Commerce, the MBDA is the only federal agency dedicated to supporting the growth and competitiveness of minority-owned businesses.

National Federation of Independent Business

(800) 634-2669
email: contact via website form
website: nfib.com

The nonprofit and nonpartisan NFIB advocates for small and independent business owners in Washington, DC, as well as in the state capitals.

National Restaurant Association

2055 L Street NW
Suite 700
Washington, DC 20036
(202) 331-5900 or (800) 424-5156
email: askus@restaurant.org
website: restaurant.org

As the largest food service trade association in the world, the National Restaurant Association represents more than 500,000 restaurants.

National Small Business Association

1156 15th Street South
Suite 502
Washington, DC 20005
(800) 345-6728
email: press@nsba.biz
website: nsba.biz

The NSBA is a nonpartisan organization that provides information, resources, and advocacy to small business owners in every state and every industry in the United States.

Score Association

1165 Herndon Parkway
Suite 100
Herndon, VA 20170
(800) 634-0245
email: help@score.org
website: score.org

The Score Association is a network of volunteer business mentors. They help entrepreneurs at any stage of their business.

Service Employees International Union

1800 Massachusetts Avenue NW
Washington, DC 20036
(202) 730-7000
email: contact via website form
website: seiu.org

The SEIU is a labor union that represents two million workers in service industries such as health care (including hospital, nursing home, and home care workers), public services (government employees, including law enforcement), and property services (janitors, security guards, etc.). The SEIU is one of the leading organizations in the fight for an increased minimum wage.

United for a Fair Economy

1 Milk Street, 5th Floor
Boston, MA 02109
(617) 423-2148
email: info@faireconomy.org
website: faireconomy.org

United for a Fair Economy uses economics education, training, and creative communications to support social movements that work for a resilient, sustainable, and equitable economy.

Unite Here

275 7th Avenue, 16th Floor
New York, NY 10001-6708
(212) 265-7000
email: contact via website form
website: unitehere.org

Unite Here is a labor union representing workers in the hotel, gaming, food service, manufacturing, textile, distribution, laundry, transportation, and airport industries in the United States and Canada.

Women's Business Development Center

8 South Michigan Avenue
4th Floor
Chicago, IL 60603
(312) 853-3477
email: wbdc@wbdc.org
website: wbdc.org

The WBDC is an organization dedicated to supporting and increasing women's business ownership and strengthening the impact of women on the economy.

Bibliography of Books

Sasha Abramsky. *The American Way of Poverty: How the Other Half Still Lives.* New York, NY: Nation, 2013.

Jessica Bruder. *Nomadland: Surviving America in the Twenty-first Century.* New York, NY: W. W. Norton, 2017.

David Card and Alan B. Krueger. *Myth and Measurement: The New Economics of the Minimum Wage* (20th Anniversary Edition). Princeton, NJ: Princeton University Press, 2016.

Matthew Desmond. *Evicted: Poverty and Profit in the American City.* New York, NY: Penguin, 2017.

Tamara Draut. *Sleeping Giant: How the New Working Class Will Transform America.* New York, NY: Doubleday, 2016.

Kathryn J. Edin and H. Luke Shaefer. *$2 a Day: Living on Almost Nothing in America.* Boston, MA: Mariner, 2016.

Barbara Ehrenreich. *Nickle and Dimed: On (Not) Getting By in America.* New York, NY: Holt, 2001.

John Freeman. *Tales of Two Americas: Stories of Inequality in a Divided Nation.* New York, NY: Penguin, 2017.

Joanne Samuel Goldblum and Colleen Shaddox. *Broke in America: Seeing, Understanding, and Ending US Poverty.* Dallas, TX: BenBella, 2021.

Emily Guendelsberger. *On the Clock: What Low Wage Work Did to Me and How It Drives America Insane.* New York, NY: Back Bay Books, 2019.

Saru Jayaraman. *Forked: A New Standard for American Dining.* New York, NY: Oxford University Press, 2016.

Saru Jayaraman. *One Fair Wage: Ending Subminimum Pay in America.* New York, NY: New Press, 2021.

Priscilla Murolo and A. B. Chitty. *From the Folks Who Brought You the Weekend: A Short Illustrated History of Labor in the United States.* New York, NY: The New Press, 2018.

Keith Payne. *The Broken Ladder: How Inequality Affects How We Think, Live, and Die.* New York, NY: Penguin, 2018.

Mark Robert Rank, et al. *Poorly Understood: What America Gets Wrong About Poverty.* New York, NY: Oxford University Press, 2021.

David Rolf. *The Fight for Fifteen: The Right Wage for a Working America.* New York, NY: The New Press, 2016.

Joseph E. Stiglitz. *People, Power, and Profits: Progressive Capitalism for an Age of Discontent.* New York, NY: W. W. Norton, 2019.

Hadas Thier. *A People's Guide to Capitalism: An Introduction to Marxist Economics.* Chicago, IL: Haymarket, 2020.

Linda Tirado. *Hand to Mouth: Living in Bootstrap America.* New York, NY: Berkeley, 2014.

Isabel Wilkerson. *Caste: The Origins of Our Discontents.* New York, NY: Random House, 2020.

Index